DAVID LETTERMAN: " TRYING TO ~~HURT PEOPLE~~, ARE YOU?"

BOZ: "YUP."

A Few of the 10 Boz Commandments:

Be yourself or be dead.

Cause change.

Show some emotion.

Never, ever, be bored.

Some Quotes from Chairman Boz:

If you see a rule that doesn't make sense, then break it. Protest it. Get rid of it.

I'm sick of the NCAA. They prostitute players in every way possible.

Don't worry. God has paid me back for all this hell I raised ...

---

*Includes Candid Photos—
and a Brand-New Chapter Written
Especially for This Edition*

THE CRITICS ARE SHOCKED, ENRAGED, AND HOWLING WITH DELIGHT OVER
THE BOZ

"THE BEST FOOTBALL BOOK OF THE 1980s . . . The Boz is not concerned with pleading his case. He's just telling his story, without apology . . . His criticisms of the National Collegiate Athletic Association are right on target . . . WOULD MAKE HUNTER THOMPSON PROUD."

—San Jose Mercury News

"IF YOU MUST BUY THIS BOOK, BE SURE YOU TAKE IT HOME IN A BROWN WRAPPER . . . We're talking drugs, sex and total lack of respect for authority here!"

—Cleveland Plain Dealer

"A SHOOT-FROM-THE-HIP, GO-FOR-THE-HEAD LINE-BACKER . . . Bosworth brags . . . boasts . . . and spends a couple of chapters trashing the league!"

—Santa Rosa Press

"THE BOZ IS OUTRAGEOUS AND OUTSPOKEN . . . Bosworth ought to be commended for putting enough of both the good and bad of himself in for readers to decide for themselves whether they like him or not . . . ENTERTAINING."

—Sacramento Union

"THE BOZ WILL SAY ANYTHING HE WANTS, ANY TIME HE WANTS . . . His book is sure to spark repercussions—investigations, lawsuits and the like. It is also sure to spark explosive sales at the bookstand!"

—Omaha World-Herald

"TAKING THIS GUY SERIOUSLY COULD BE HARMFUL TO YOUR HEALTH."

—Tulsa World

**A Choice of The Literary Guild
and Doubleday Book Club
Serialized in *Rolling Stone***

BRIAN BOSWORTH
with
Rick Reilly

CONFESSIONS OF A MODERN ANTI-HERO

THE

CHARTER BOOKS, NEW YORK

This Charter book contains the updated
text of the original hardcover edition.
It has been completely reset in a typeface
designed for easy reading, and was printed
from new film.

THE BOZ:
CONFESSIONS OF A MODERN ANTI-HERO

A Charter Book / published by arrangement with
Doubleday, a division of Bantam Doubleday
Dell Publishing Group, Inc.

PRINTING HISTORY
Doubleday edition / September 1988
Charter edition / September 1989

ISBN: 1-55773-248-5

Charter Books are published by The Berkley Publishing Group,
200 Madison Avenue, New York, New York 10016.
The name "CHARTER" and the "C" logo
are trademarks belonging to Charter Communications, Inc.

PRINTED IN THE UNITED STATES OF AMERICA

10 9 8 7 6 5 4 3 2 1

To my father, whose perseverance and guidance helps me endure.

—BRIAN BOSWORTH

To Jim and Jan Campbell, whose secret hideaway helped us get it done and whose daughter makes it all worthwhile.

—RICK REILLY

CONTENTS

1 Finally, First 1

2 Off the Top of My Head 17

3 Football by Bozmosis 35

4 Pranks for the Memories 53

5 Life Without Rules 71

6 A Few Screws Loose 91

7 Say It's So, Joe 109

8 The World According to Me 127

9 Fame, Fortune, and Females 149

10 Miami Twice 169

11 Hello, Moscow 189

12 The King and I 207

13 55 Minus 44 Equals
11 Million 225

14 They Shoot Linebackers,
Don't They? 245

15 The Last Picture Show 265

16 The World's Largest
Book-Eating Party 277

**CONFESSIONS
OF A MODERN
ANTI-HERO**

THE

CHAPTER
1

Finally, First

Miami. The Orange Bowl. New Year's Night, 1986. And I'm standing on the field between plays, peeling a huge chunk of skin out of my hand and grinning. I'm not talking about a little skin. I'm talking about *layers* of skin, a big gouge of skin the size of a big broken rubber band. And it feels good. It hurts like hell, but it feels good. In fact, it feels great. The more skin, the better.

I guess some people think that I'd be a good subject for *Halloween 4* or something, but I've always liked pain that way. Pain and blood let you know you're playing serious football. Let you know you're not dogging it, that you're into the game. Whenever I'm playing really well, I'm bashing people with my fists, cutting my hands up on their helmets—a bad-ass Cuisinart pureeing people into vegetables. If I'm really into it, I can't even feel the gash until I look down at my hands later and notice that half of them are gone. Those are the best kind—when you cut the skin so deep it doesn't even bleed.

Right then—standing there, holding a big wad of skin in my hand—was the first time it hit me that we were national champions. And that night, in front of my favorite people in the world, the good and upstanding citizens of Miami, Florida (those that aren't

in jail), I felt like I'd finally accomplished something. I'd just won a national championship ring.
Not that I'd ever actually *wear* the thing. For one
thing, it's so huge it spreads your fingers apart so
you feel like you're giving the sign of Vulcan. You
wear it on your right hand and you walk around with
a tilt like the Elephant Man. Besides, it's too gaudy,
too much like something our coach, Barry Switzer,
would wear. Geez, there I go. And I promised I
wouldn't jump on The King.

That's what we called Switzer, The King, because he ruled over the University of Oklahoma and
the world of college football. Or he did until he
signed a dumb-looking white high school linebacker
out of Irving, Texas, who had a brain and a plan.
But I'm getting ahead of myself. Or is it behind?

Anyway, I knew I'd left everything I had on the
field when I walked off it that night. I remembered
afterward, I was so sore that I couldn't walk, couldn't
sleep, couldn't lie on my back, couldn't lie on my
side, couldn't do nothing. I was a poster child for
months afterward. Some things have never quite
healed. It still takes me about five minutes to get my
coat on because it's almost impossible for me to turn
my shoulder a certain way. But that night was worth
it. We beat the ugly out of Penn State, which is saying something, as ugly as those guys are in their
Stalag 17 uniforms. Those uniforms must've been
picked out by their coach, Joe Paterno, Mr. Blue
Light Special himself. "Hey, Joe, we're driving by
another Target. Wanna pick out a new suit?"

Joe's Choirboys and the University of Oklahoma
football team didn't make much of a match. Whoever decided to put us together in Miami for ten

days—at the same hotel, no less—must've been in a straitjacket. Joe brought all his players down to Miami in blue blazers and ugly rep ties and penny loafers to match their perfect little 11–0 record, waged against fierce teams like Rutgers and Temple. Penn State didn't have a hair or a word out of place that whole week.

Meanwhile, I got off the plane in army fatigues (a little number designed by Oscar de la ROTC). My buddy Paul Migliazzo wore a pair of jeans ripped from the cuff to the hip and held together by about a thousand safety pins. A lot of the guys wore some scary stuff, too, a lot of gold chains and $300 sweatsuits and Reeboks. And, of course, shades— standard. Standing on the tarmac that day, we must've looked like we took a wrong turn at Hollywood and Vine. We were the exact kind of people your mother said not to hang out with. We were The Wrong Crowd.

Before that game, Joe jumped our case—especially *my* case—one day at a press conference, saying *his* players would never dress like that, be outrageous, say outlandish things, try to stand out. What he really wanted to do was point at my hair and say, "And we'd *kill* them before we'd let them wear their hair like that Satan worshipper." But I know some guys at Penn State and I think a lot of them would have liked to have been allowed to be themselves, which is all I ever wanted to be. They would've liked to wear their hair the way they wanted to, dress how they felt like, say what they wanted to. It's just that Joe's got everybody up there brainwashed into thinking you have to look the same and dress the same and talk the same and stare at your shoes and light a candle at Joe's shrine. Bless you. Take a lap.

He's a great coach and everything, I don't deny him that, but I never thought it was right for him to say that about us. In fact, I thought it was classless as hell, trying to point fingers at our players. Look, Joe Pa, don't argue with our success and we won't argue with yours. Try not to judge others and they won't judge you. Nice pants. Get that flooded basement taken care of?

The only thing I liked about Penn State at all were those big black high-top football shoes. Some people hate them. I like them. I like to wear big black high-top Reeboks myself sometimes in the summer, with white socks, white shorts, and a white T-shirt that says something like EAT ME. Freaks old women out in malls.

But the funny thing about all this holier-than-thou bull that Penn State was laying on the press down there was that, really, the roles were the opposite of what they seemed. We were the ones drinking Perrier and lime and they were the ones sucking down every piña colada in sight. We were the ones in bed by ten and they were the ones trying to get into Miss Orange Bowl's royal underwear. We were the ones who had gotten down there five days early and had made a commitment to winning. And we were the ones sitting back, laughing at all those morons getting plastered every night, because we knew exactly what was going to happen.

See, we had screwed up the year before just like they were about to screw up. We had come down to the Orange Bowl as Big Eight champions and that was as far as we wanted our season to go. It was my freshman year and Oklahoma hadn't been Big Eight champs in four years. Getting that title back that year was the end of our rainbow. Everything else was gravy, even though we could've won a national championship by beating Washington that year. Looking back on it, with the team we had, we could've kicked Washington's ass. But that was beyond our goal. We set our goal too low and went to Miami to celebrate. We hit up every party and every function and every girl and every no-cash bar. When the hangover finally lifted, we realized we blew it. And we vowed to never do it again.

In fact, when we knew we were going to Miami to play Penn State for the title the next year, I called a team meeting. I said, "Look, when we were down there last year, we jacked around and played like shit and we felt like shit all year long. We had to live that loss down and there ain't nothing worse than ending the season on a loss because that's all you get to remember for a whole year."

We'd been through a ton of trouble just to get where we were. The seniors had finally given us sophomores control of the team and I didn't want to blow it. We'd lost our starting quarterback, Troy Aikman, found a better one, Jamelle Holieway, lost to Vinny Testaverde and Miami early in the season, but then beat some good teams—Nebraska, Oklahoma State, and SMU—and got back to number two. And when Miami lost to the University of Florida, we were given a reprieve. We had a chance to make up for Washington. And all of us knew we weren't going to louse it up this time.

"Now we need to make a commitment to ourselves," I said. "We'll celebrate after the game . . .

ain't no drinking . . . ain't going down there to party
. . . ain't going down there to screw girls. Just going
down there to take care of business. And then, after
we win, we'll be back here and celebrate. *Then* we'll
drink, party, and screw girls!'' I should've been in
politics.

But I was going to be damned if I wasn't going to
set an example. I had my own strict game plan. No
drinking, no partying, and, most of all, no sex for
the whole two weeks. During the season, I always
cut off sex on Thursday before the game (Friday in
the pros). I just do. I feel more aggressive that way.
Kathleen Turner could come up to me stark naked
the day before a game and blow in my ear and I
wouldn't so much as twitch. For the Orange Bowl,
I decided to avoid intimacy for the whole time I was
down there. We went five days before Christmas, so
that's a long time. And believe me, did my girlfriend
ever tempt me. Did she *ever*.

My girlfriend came down for the whole ten days
and I kept things on a platonic level the whole time.
Boy, if you'd ever seen her, you'd know I deserve
some kind of Nobel Prize for that. I was serious
about winning. I wanted to win that game more than
anything in the world. I wanted OU to be national
champions.

We were like those guys in *The Blues Brothers*.
We were on a mission from God. We were driven.
Oklahoma hadn't won a national championship since
1975 and we wanted to be there when they put up
1985 on the scoreboard to go with the five others.
I'll never forget walking into that stadium the first
time and seeing all those national championships up

there. It gave me chills, and I don't chill easily. I wanted to put one up myself.

We missed Christmas at home and nobody even bitched. We went through two-a-days all over again, if you can believe that. Usually, you go through two-a-days in the summer and thank God you never have to see the sons of bitches again. But we agreed to do it so that we could get used to the Miami humidity, which is brutal. And nobody bitched about that either. We'd practice in the morning in full pads, and then we wouldn't even go anywhere for lunch. They packed us our lunch and we just sat down right there and ate it on the practice field. Then we practiced in the afternoon in full pads. Even in the summer, you only do one of the two practices in full pads. We did that for five days. And what were the Eagle Scouts doing? Practicing once a day and hitting the umbrella drinks at night. The only people hitting the bars on our team were the assistant coaches. God knows where The King was. I never saw him.

Unfortunately, I had to see all those Beaver Cleavers from Penn State constantly. Plenty of times we were *required* to go to functions with those jokers. I'll never understand that. No offense, but I don't feel like being best buddies with somebody who I'm planning to jack in the teeth the next day. I don't like exchanging addresses with somebody I'm fixing to get in a fight with. I don't want to know 'em. I might like 'em, and I don't want to like anybody before a game, not them, not the refs, not even my own teammates. I'll talk to them after the game.

Penn State didn't see it my way, though. They kept calling me names, saying "Say, man, what the hell is wrong with *you*? Why don't you talk to us? Too good for us, man?''

And I'd say, "I just have nothing to say to you. You go your own way and I'll see you in the Orange Bowl. That's when I'll have a few things to say."

So I went to these functions in what you'd call an ornery mood. I didn't talk to anybody. They tried to talk to me, but I just kept right on walking. One time, on this boat we were all on, some dinner or something, one of their strength coaches came up. I was standing by our coaches while they were playing blackjack and this drunk idiot tries to come up and talk to me. Just trying to bull with me.

"Excuse me, but I'm not in the mood to talk to you right now," I said.

So he left and then came back with two meathead players of his. He was talking real loud and he said, "Hey, Boz, this is what a real linebacker looks like."

So I start over to them to have a little chat with them. But then my strength coach, Pete Martinelli, grabs me.

"You can't get into a fight!" he's yelling at me. "Don't worry about it. We'll take care of it on the field. It ain't worth it."

So I step back and what does Pete do? He jumps their ass! "You bleeping bleeps!" He starts shoving, daring guys to throw punches. Pete is just a little guy, but I know I'd never fight him. "You get the bleep out of here."

I turned to Pete and said, "Thanks for showing me how to restrain myself."

I was outraged about it for a while, ready to punch anybody wearing an ugly uniform, but then we realized what they were doing. They were all blitzed.

One guy was throwing up over the railing. And we were laughing hilariously at what was about to happen.

So what happened? On the very first series of the game, they drove the whole damn field and scored a rushing touchdown. That chapped my ass. We'd only given up four rushing touchdowns *the whole year*. And now we gave one up right away to these knuckleheads? All of a sudden, we were behind, 7–0. We came off the field and we're going, "What the hell is going on?"

I got on the phone with our defensive coordinator, Gary Gibbs, the best coach in America without a head coaching job, and Gibbs told me to calm down. "We're all right," he said. "Let's see what happens this series."

And we were all right. We went out there and gave them our motto for that year: "Three and out." Which means first down, second down, third down, and then we're out, our defense is off the field. Time for the other team to punt. "Three and out." I love to hear those words. "Got nothing for your highlight reel here. Now get your widebody ass off the field."

Tim Lashar, our buffed-up field goal kicker, got a quick three for us. When we got it back, Joe the Genius did something really stupid. We had a third and twenty-four at our own twenty-nine, so what do the Nitwit Nittanies do? They blitzed. Jamelle audibled at the line and sent Keith Jackson long. Keith made a stupendous play, a seventy-one-yard touchdown, to give us the lead, 10–7. We only threw six passes the whole game, but we only needed to throw that one. Keith must have been the greatest tight end in the world playing in the dumbest place. Why'd he choose Oklahoma, where the forward pass is thrown about every eclipse? I have no idea. It's like a Scotch drinker picking BYU. All I know is I'm glad he did. He'd get the ball about three times a game and score twice and complain about not having a chance at the Heisman the rest of the time.

Lashar booted a couple more field goals and Sonny Brown, one of the world's only white cornerbacks, got an interception before halftime and so did Tony Rayburn. But their kicker got a field goal just before halftime and we only led by six, 16–10. But it didn't seem that close to me. We'd shut their faces down since the first touchdown drive.

Okay, I'll give them a little credit. They came back and took it to our one-yard line before Sonny (thank you, Sonny) got another interception. Then Lashar got another field goal to make it 19–10 and it was all over. Right about then is when I got in the greatest hit of my life.

The Cleaver Family was trying to run some kind of backyard bullshit shuffle pass. I guess they thought it would be cute. They pulled one of their fat-ass offensive linemen up in the hole, but he totally ignored me. I went by him like the 5:15. I caught the fullback flush in midstride. Right in the stomach. Some friends of mine said you could hear the pop in the top rows. And then I kept right on going. I just kept driving his head into the ground. He looked like a farm plow, his helmet just plowing up the field. I think we'll plant carrots here.

And, typical Penn State, the fat-ass lineman that missed me came up after that hit and said, ''Well, it's about time you hit somebody.''

Right. ''Oh, you've been out here a long bleeping

time,'' I yelled. ''Your mom won't even have to clean that ugly uniform you're wearing. You've played a great game, haven't you? Aren't you late for your seventh meal of the day?''

A few minutes later we got another touchdown to make it 25–10 and that was the end. It sunk in. We were national champs. And I looked around the locker room and saw all these guys that I'd lived with and eaten with and drank with and fought with and chased nags with. They looked like the party scene from *One Flew Over the Cuckoo's Nest*. There was the human condo Stevie Bryan, our defensive end. He was the brother of Ricky and Mitch and not one of them was under 260 pounds. Nicest brothers you've ever met, but considering they had to live with each other, they're lucky to be alive. They grew up on a farm and when they'd get mad at each other, they'd throw hay bales at each other. Do you know how heavy a hay bale is? At OU they used to throw knives at each other and stab each other on purpose. I remember sitting in the cafeteria and they'd be stabbing each other in the back of the leg. One time, when they were kids, Stevie threw a knife at Mitch and stabbed him so bad that he was sure his dad was going to beat the hell out of him, so he ran away from home. He finally came back and his dad beat the hell out of him anyway.

There was Richard Reed, our other defensive end, who was hilarious because he's this big old jelly ass. I mean, looking at him, he didn't look like a football player, he looked like the Fuji blimp. But he played like hell.

Some guys that were important to me weren't even starters. Like my backup, Evan Gatewood, the next

President of the United States. That's what we always called him because all of us are sure he'll be President. He's the smartest guy I've ever met and had the best study habits of anybody. He gave college football a serious bad name. Therefore, I devoted my life to corrupting him. One time, on the way home from the Texas game, we got stuck in traffic, and we just *happened* to have a bunch of eggs back there. We weren't supposed to, but we did. So we started heaving these eggs into the traffic. We even got Evan to do it. Imagine that, we were ruining the next President of the United States. Someday Gatewood's going to be President and I'm going to walk into his office and say, "All right, Evan. Either give me the ambassadorship to Tahiti or I tell the world about the eggs."

Spencer Tillman was a black running back who sounded like a white English dean. He was a broadcast major and was very literate. Spencer always *ar-tic-u-la-ted* his words very carefully and correctly. He was real serious, very businesslike. I probably respected him more than anybody on the team. He wasn't two-faced. He was up on everything. He was telling me how I was doing in the Butkus Award—the award I won twice as best linebacker in the country—before I even knew what the hell a Butkus Award was.

Mig was probably my favorite guy, Paul Migliazzo. Mig was like me. He gets bored easily, so he does whatever he can to spice up life. Like on picture day he wore his hair in some demented Jamaican Jah Love 'do, with two watches on each arm and rings on every finger. He didn't take a shower or comb his hair. He looked like hell. And he's meeting all the fans and signing autographs and getting his picture taken with them. The fans must've thought, "And we thought Bob Marley was dead." And he did it just to piss the coaches off. He even wore a camera around his neck for the team picture. And you'll notice in the picture that while he's smiling, he's trying to push me off the back of the top row of the bleachers. My best pal.

Then there was Sonny, the most famous man in Alice, Texas. He loved to drink tequila, but he hated to do laundry. Sonny is the only man in existence who operates on the Smell-Pile principle. What he'd do is, all week he'd throw his clothes into a pile in the middle of his room. Then, when he ran out of clothes, he'd go to the pile and smell 'em. The ones that he figured smelled all right, he'd wear again. The ones that smelled bad, he'd turn inside out and wear. Luckily, I knew all about the Smell-Pile principle. Any time I'd see Sonny wearing clothes inside out, I'd get out the Lysol.

Sonny's real name was Clifton Doyle Brown and boy did that piss him off. So I always called him Clifton. Tannest guy of non-Mexican descent I've ever met.

And then I looked over and saw our leader, The King, getting a serious case of the hugs. He's hugging everybody. He's about to hurt himself. If Switzer is one thing—and he's a lot of things, which we'll talk about later—he's emotional. This was his third national championship, putting him up on that big platform with some biggies like Bear Bryant—and he was eating it up. I felt really close to him then. As things would turn out, that was really the last time.

Me, I was happy as hell. Happier. Dad came in to the locker room and I remember almost crying. Dad did everything for me growing up, but he was a hard guy to satisfy. Second was never good enough for him. Come to think of it, sometimes first wasn't good enough either. But this first was good enough. I could tell that in his face.

Then I looked up from hugging him and there were about thirteen jillion reporters waiting for me. I guess I'd had a pretty good game. The defense played great, held them to ten first downs, and I'd had thirteen solo tackles. Reporters had been hitting on me all week, but now they seemed to want to know *everything*. And, always happy to be of help, I started telling them everything.

And as they were scribbling and I was talking, I remember, in the middle of it, thinking, "Nothing is going to be quite the same after this, is it?"

I was right. I just didn't know how right.

CHAPTER
2

Off the Top
of My Head

All right, I'll admit it. You see the way I wear my hair? It's not just a haircut. It's the secret international sign of the Anti-Christ Club of America. It's how all of us in our devil worshippers' cult wear it. We meet every Thursday night behind the Elks lodge in Peoria, Illinois. Everybody does a dance with a blow dryer in one hand and a jar of mousse in the other. Qaddafi comes a lot too. What you see him wear on television is just a toupee. He really wears The Boz underneath.

I mean, so many people want to believe that about my hair I figure I might as well let them die in peace. One time a reporter came up to me and asked where I get my designs for the side of my head.

"Out of *The Book of Black Magic*," I said.

And he wrote down every word. Had a real scoop.

I can't tell you how many people come up to me and say, "Look at you. Look at your hair. Imagine what God must think of you."

Yeah, I can imagine God spends his whole day thinking about my hair. "Geez, look at Boz. Wearing his hair straight up on the top and shaved on the side. And check out that tail. That's it. Hey, Jesus, get me a plague or something I can set on this moron. Hey, wait a minute, Jesus. You kinda need a

19

haircut too." Let me ask you this. You think God likes Jim Bakker's hair much? Or Jimmy Swaggart's? It's like: "Well, you guys have probably cheated people out of money and sinned and hung out with prostitutes and everything else, but it's okay with me. Your hair is just the way I like it."

Personally, I like my hair. I think it looks good on me. I *really* like it. Someone asked me once, if I lived all alone on an island where no one could ever see me, would I wear my hair like this? And I said, "Yeah. Would you wear your hair the way you wear it?" You wear your hair the way you do because you like it like that. You're not doing it under gunpoint or something, although people have asked me if I lost a bet.

Why do people take it upon themselves to worry about my hair? I don't worry about it. Why should they? Aren't there enough interesting things going on in their own lives that they've got to worry about my hair? I don't give a rat's ass what people think about my hair anyway. This is how I want to look. I think I look good. It's easy to take care of. It's comfortable. It feels right on me.

More than anything, it's a way to express my individuality. It's a way to show that I don't buy The Established Way of Doing Things—conformity. It makes me happy. I modify it all the time—long, short, long tail, no tail, different designs and stripes. I don't want anyone getting an edge on me.

I mean, everybody on the whole damn planet walks around with their hair almost exactly alike. They dress alike and think alike and shop at the same places and it drives me crazy. It's like they all got churned out of the same boring factory. "Beep. Another businessman. Gray pin-striped suit. White shirt. Red-print tie. Brylcreem haircut. Brunette wife. Two-point-four kids. Beep. Next.'' I want to do something different. Who wants to be a sheep?

It's hilarious, though, I think. Because they used to scream at kids for wearing their hair long. ''Get a damn haircut!'' they'd say. Now they're wearing it like me, short as can be, and now they're still screaming at kids. ''Let your hair grow out!'' How are kids supposed to know what to do? Adults are so screwed up. There's no pleasing them. They don't know what they want. Except two things: (1) they don't want you being any different than anybody else on the block; and (2) they want to yell at you.

Now a few hair-grooming pointers: just because The Boz looks good on me doesn't mean it looks good on *you*. I mean, they call it The Boz because it fits me. They don't call it The O'Sullivan or The Finkelstein. Some people it looks good on. And some people it looks downright scary on.

One time I saw it on a grandmother. I'm serious. It almost made me shave my head. It was during the NFL strike in 1987 in Seattle. We wanted to get the fans on our side, so we held a little rally that Kenny Easley put together. I personally was against it. It's like I told Kenny: ''You think it's a good idea to let the fans have free run at us?'' After all, some of the fans were totally pissed off at us. I was thinking that somebody might bring a shotgun.

I went anyway, like an idiot. I was one of about ten suckers there and, of course, I got mobbed. I got stuck signing autographs for four hours. I was pinned against a Chevy Luv pickup truck and finally I had to jump into the bed of it. And I yelled at everybody, "I'm not signing anything else until everybody gets in line!" I thought I might not get out of there alive otherwise. You should've seen that line. It was a mile long. My hand hurt for a day after that.

Anyway, this lady comes up who must've been in her late sixties and as soon as I saw her I said to myself, "I don't believe this." She had her hair painted all in colors. She even had the big Seahawk on the side of her head. I'm telling you the truth. But I don't know. As bad as she looked, at least she must've given the old codgers a rise at the Senior Citizens' Center. Then again, I guess they've already got a bunch of bluehairs down there as it is.

See, I have a square head. The Boz looks good on square heads. But I've seen a million kids—and adults—with round heads or oval heads wearing The Boz anyway. I've seen some kids who are just unbelievably bad-looking in it. I feel sorry for them, I really do.

It's like the kid who came up to me one day after a Seahawk game wearing The Boz. I asked him if he liked his haircut.

"Nope," he said.

"How come?" I said.

"My mother made me get it."

You've got to feel sorry for that kid. If his mother wanted to look like a dweeb so bad, why didn't she get one herself? Let her poor offspring alone.

The whole thing started, really, in high school. It was a tradition that everybody would go down before the season and get a burr cut. I'd tell Dad that I was going to go down and get a burr cut and he'd always say, "The hell you are, you ain't getting no burr cut. You get a burr cut, don't you come back to this

house.'' I don't know why he had such a red ass for
burr cuts, but I had to live by that rule. At the same
time, I wasn't too keen on the idea anyway. I never
really wanted to look like Ozzie Nelson. So everybody on my team had strange hair and I didn't. I
guess I stand out one way or the other.

So then I get to Oklahoma and I really didn't think
about doing it. I had normal everyday Joe Blow factory hair. I don't know what I was thinking back
then, but I looked like a real Gomer. I'd wear these
awful stretch denim pants that had a zip fly and these
nasty-looking plaid wool shirts. I'd wear those shirts
really tight. Don't ask me why. The buttons would
be ready to burst. I guess that's how I told people,
''I lift weights'' or something juvenile like that. I
wore cowboy boots. And I had sort of goofball sideburns—long motorcycle sideburns—that look really
attractive. It's amazing I ever met a girl. But I grew
out of it. Half the white guys in the NFL still dress
like that.

So what happened was that Mig—my linebacking
buddy at Oklahoma, Paul Migliazzo—got his hair
cut one day by a woman named Camille Benso. And,
to tell you the truth, it was an ugly haircut. It was
just stupid. It was combed at the top and cut real
strange on the sides. It was layered, if you can believe that. It looked like he'd gotten it cut in Moscow
or something for two rubles.

I just looked at him and said, ''Paul, what the *hell*
did you do to your hair?''

''Well,'' he said. ''We got started and when we
finished this is what was left.''

Nice. But then he kept ragging on me to get my
hair cut by the same girl. Return to the scene of the

crime, sort of. He said if I went in, his next one is free.

"Real smart, Mig. That's like going to a restaurant, getting food poisoning, and then going back there because they gave you a half-off coupon."

So how come I let myself get talked into it? I don't know. Actually, I do know. It was after the season-opening game of my sophomore year. We'd barely beaten Minnesota, 13-7, and I'd played like dogshit. My ankle was still hurting from when I'd sprained it badly way back the spring before and I was feeling depressed and I just decided I needed to change *something*. I wanted something new. I needed some kind of motivation to get me going. So I guess you could say my haircut is a statement of rage. It had nothing to do with getting attention. I did it to change my way of thinking, to shake myself up, to make me look at things in a different way, to make me look at *myself* in a different way. I've always been like that. I've always motivated myself. Nobody else could.

So I took a big swallow and walked into Camille's place, petrified. I sat down, and she said, "Well, what do you want to do to it?"

"I have no idea."

"Well, we could do this"—and she shows me a picture in a magazine—"or we could do that." Another picture.

"Well, how about if you cut if all off and make it stand up at the top?"

"Your hair won't do that."

"Well, how about if you just cut it all off on the sides and make it stand up like that?"

"Your hair won't do that either. I'd have to just

cut it all the way down and train it as it grows back up.''

So I said, ''Well, I guess my hair is in training then.''

So she cut it all off and I said, ''That's pretty good. How am I gonna keep it like that?'' Really, it looked like a burr the first time we did it. And I started laughing about it because I wondered how I was going to get back into my own house when I went home to Irving. Dad saw me later that week at the game, standing on the sideline with my helmet off.

Afterward, he came up and said, ''What the hell did you do to your hair?'' Popular question.

''Well,'' I said. ''Considering I don't live in your house anymore, I went and cut the shit off.''

Every week I'd go to Camille's after that and every week we kind of modified it, doing different things to it every time until it finally evolved into what it is now. There you have it: from ape to man.

Later on we started letting it grow really full on top and shaving it really close on the sides. I had told her I wanted a much more defined look. She just cut it straight off at the top and took it off clean at the sides, and we kept it like that for the rest of that year.

So we talked all the next summer about what our next creation was going to be and we couldn't think of anything we both liked. The season opener was coming up—UCLA at home—and I was getting real nervous. I had to do something different. It was starting to be like a superstition. And nobody's more superstitious than me.

''Why don't you just put some stripes in the

side?'' I said. Camille was kind of flabbergasted, but she did it, except you couldn't see them.

"Can you color them?''

And she did that, and she liked it so much that she said, ''Well, let's try a bunch of colors in there.''

And I said, ''No way. I'm not walking around with a bunch of colors in my hair.''

But I walked out of that place with a bunch of colors in my hair. I felt like, ''Oh Christ, I'm walking around Norman, Oklahoma, with most of the colors of the rainbow on the sides of my head. Not just one color, but four.'' I felt like one of those guys who hold up the JOHN 3:16 sign at sporting events. I really didn't know what to think about it.

I decided to get the worst part over with. So I went straight from Camille's to the football locker room. I walked in and just kind of walked around and everybody just kind of stopped and looked and then, pretty soon, all the black guys were going, ''Hey, man, that's cool as hell.'' And all the white guys were asking the $64,000 Question: ''What the *hell* did you do to your hair?''

The black guys liked it. The white guys hated it. It was right then that I knew it was good. White guys have no style.

In fact, the black guys liked it so much they started putting stripes in *their* hair. So then I put my number, 44, in the side and dyed it and they started doing it too. This is how the Green Bay Packers became great, I'm telling you.

I'm not sure what happened after that except this haircut of mine started exploding on top of people's heads all over the country. It was a weird feeling, though, because so many people look like turds in it. Then somebody started calling it The Boz. I didn't do it. People think I decided one day, "Okay, let's call this thing The Boz." I have no idea how it happened.

My dad was in a Sears store in Irving, Texas, where I grew up, when he saw a kid with a haircut like mine for the first time. He said, "Where'd you get that haircut, son?"

"Oh man, this is The Boz!" the kid said. "Everybody's got one!"

Dad thought the Earth was being invaded. Personally, I like it a lot better than a ROZELLE headband.

The madness was everywhere. One day I saw a newspaper picture of an entire high school team wearing it—the Clayton, Georgia, Wildcats. And every man to a Wildcat had their hair cut like me. They told me the barber had to stay open until ten o'clock to get it done. I think it would've been funny to take that whole team into Rozelle's home late at night—very quietly—and stand them all by his bed and then he'd wake up and think he was having the worst nightmare of his life—the world was being overrun by tiny Bozzes. He'd be so scared he'd lose his tan.

Anyway, somebody called me and asked if I could write the Wildcats and give them some incentive. But I did better than that. I called. Twenty of the boys went over to this lady's house for a movie and dinner the night before their big game. I have no idea how she could tell them apart, but I guess she did. So I called and talked to the captain, a kid named Vance Gillespie. I told him as captain it was his job to get his team ready. I told him to win and to win with pride. I told them to play with all their hearts and leave everything they had on the field.

Under my inspirational guidance they promptly went out and lost, 24–17.

But that didn't kill the tide. I'm sure if I'd have showed up with my hair shaped like a Hoover vacuum cleaner, some team in Mississippi would've done the same thing. Actually, when I think back on some of the things Camille *wanted* to do, I'm surprised she didn't think of that. She thought of everything else.

One time she wanted to shave one side down and let the other side grow out. She said it would look great. "A slope!" she said. Or one time she wanted me to have the middle go straight up, about a foot. I said, "Right. And then I'll move to London." One time I wanted to shave the top down and let the sides grow out, but she convinced me it would look like I'd been attacked by a Toro.

The only thing I don't like about my hair is the fact that girls feel like they always have to come up and touch it. I hate that. I'm not some museum piece. I'm not a fur coat. Keep your damn hands to yourself. If I want to be stroked, I'll call you. I'm sure you've got an 800 number.

Camille got kind of famous out of all this. She loved it when reporters would call her, asking her all the hows and whys. She'd get real possessive about it too. Like: "Screw it. It's my haircut and no one is gonna cut the thing but me. I'm gonna patent it."

Fat chance. Do you know how many quote un-quote celebrities have copied it? I mean, look at the Denver Broncos' wide receiver Vance Johnson. All of a sudden he's got a haircut like mine and he's calling it The Vance. Hmmmm. Wonder where he got that idea? He even wanted to dye it blond, but he was too cheap to have a professional do it, so he did it himself and screwed it up. Halfway through, it started burning his head. He rinsed it all out right then and it wound up as this sort of University of Texas puke orange. That's what you get, Amigo.

And then there's this pro wrestler Sting, whose hair is exactly like mine. Tells people it's his own idea. I should get a percentage of his gate.

And then there are the Boston Celtics. They aren't wearing their hair like mine (Thank God. The Celtics have got to be the ugliest collection of pro athletes I've ever seen), but during my rookie season with Seattle, I was wearing this strip of cloth around my head to keep the sweat out of my eyes and, just for the hell of it, it had a long tail that ran down the back of my head to the middle of my back. Well, when the Celtics came into Seattle to play the SuperSonics, they all showed up at their practice wearing the headband with the tail. Doggone coattailers.

Anyway, back to the haircut. Some people might look good in it if they weren't too cheap to get it done right. They get it done for five dollars by somebody who has no idea how to cut it. Me, I don't go for any five-dollar haircuts. I don't even go for a fifty-five-dollar haircut. In Seattle I get mine done by Jerry Callahan, who does Heart's hair. He gets me for about ninety dollars every time. And that's cheap for what he does.

It takes Jerry about one and a half to three hours to do my 'do. And I get one every week, usually on

Friday, or else it would start to look pretty shabby. During the season, it's like a superstition before a game. It's relaxing. I sit in the chair while the dye for the stripes sets. That can take a long time. I'll either sleep or read a book. I picked Jerry, oddly enough, because he didn't offer to do my hair for free. A lot of the stylists in Seattle sent me letters telling me to come in and they'd do me for free. The ones that want to do it for free usually aren't worth a damn. Jerry takes pride in his work. He's not some groupie. I think it's paid off for him too. He's been on "NFL Live" with Brent Musburger. He's done well.

We've expanded our horizons—*hair*izons?—on the sides too. We've done stripes and a diamondback symbol and some other stuff. One time, just before the Kansas City game, we did an arrowhead, but nobody in Kansas City got the joke. We've braided the tail a few times, colored it, left it long, cut it short. We've done it all. The edge.

I get the same reaction from pro players as I did from college players. The black guys on the Seahawks mostly like it and the white guys mostly hate it. Some of the white guys still wonder about it. Every time I get it done, they holler out, "Everybody come over and see what he's got in his hair this week!" Oh, sorry, guys. For some reason I don't go for that Mom-puts-a-mixing-bowl-over-it-and-gets-out-the-weed-eater look.

The other thing that the world seems to want to spend endless hours debating is my earrings. I don't know why. They're my lobes. Everybody gives me grief about my earrings. Well, not everybody. Just nerds and university presidents. (Sorry, same thing.)

I like my earrings. I wear all three on one ear. One is a little diamond stud that goes in the lobe. The other is a little gold clip that goes on top. And the third is a gold one that says BOZ and goes just below the stud—on *the* stud, meaning me, of course. The BOZ one somebody just sent me through the mail. Somebody I'd never met. Thanks very much if you're out there.

However, *how* I got the earring is not one of my fondest memories. I was blotto at this one party my sophomore year, and I told Carl Cabiness to stick an earring in my ear. No alcohol. No numbness. No nothing. And Carl, always the nice guy, was happy to oblige. He just got up and pushed it through. I heard two pops. Pop, pop. That was the cartilage in my ear busting. It felt just fine then, but it hurt like hell the next day and it got infected and stayed infected for about a month. Real genius, me. But at least I took pleasure in knowing I was the first white guy on the team to have an earring.

I borrowed my first earring from a girl at a party. Since then I've always had people make me stuff. I've had one that said 44 and I had somebody, just out of the blue, send me one that said BOZ in gold with a diamond in the middle. Again, very thoughtful.

I've taken some abuse from old farts in the press, but the young guys, the cool guys—believe it or not, there are one or two cool sportswriters out there—seem to like the look. One guy that didn't like it, I guess, was a sportswriter from *Newsday* in New York. He actually wrote an entire column about what I do when I get out of the shower.

After a game he watched everything I did. I guess

he was waiting for me to come and talk to him. He said that I: "(a) laced my torso with baby powder; (b) dressed in a stone-washed black denim suit; (c) affixed a wide gold chain around my neck; (d) put three silver earrings in my left ear—the first hoop earring went atop the ear, then the stud-pierced earring went near the middle, then the pierced earring spelling BOZ went on the lobe; (e) put on my deep-blue wraparound sunglasses to face the TV lights." I resented that. The stud-pierced earring went on the bottom. Besides, doesn't he respect a guy's privacy? What if I wrote a column about what he does after he gets out of the shower . . .

"Okay, So-and-So got out of the shower and rubbed himself with the towel. (Seemed like an extra-long time, by the way.) Then he put on the same underwear he wore yesterday. Then he put on a lime-green leisure suit. He forgot deodorant. Then he took a Bic pen to his hair to comb it. He added a pair of white socks, one with a rip in it, and then a ring he got from a box of Lucky Charms."

Wait till that sportswriter gets a load of what I want to put in next—an earring that dangles. He'll probably get a miniseries out of that.

I'm sure my mom would like to see them throw the book at me for the earrings. When she saw my earring for the first time, she told me to take it out. For people of her generation, they thought it meant you were gay or something. I told her I wouldn't take it out. I think she likes it now.

My dad had a little bit harder time with it. And not just with my hair, but my earrings and the things I said in the papers. I love him and he knows that. But he had to learn to accept me as an individual. I am not a bad person. I don't break the law, snort coke, or attack women. I've never been arrested. I had a 3.3 grade-point average in college. Just because the hair on top of my head is strange doesn't mean what's going on inside of it is wrong.

We went around and around about what I was saying and how I looked, but in the end my dad realized he had to accept me the way I was if he wanted to be my friend. And we are the best of friends. I call him and my mom all the time about everything. I'm glad it worked out that way. I refuse to live in a world full of façades. Truth is the ultimate wisdom. If you can't be yourself, you may as well die.

It's funny, but Switzer and I never had that trouble. He never questioned me over my hair or the earrings or my clothes or anything. One thing about Switzer, he let his players be who they were. He called it his "comfort zone." He let Billy Sims wear the biggest Afro in creation. He let Joe Washington wear silver shoes. He let Thomas Lott wear a headband and Jack Mildren wear his hair down the back of his neck. And he let me do just about everything else.

I know he liked the haircut and the earrings because one time he said to somebody, I can't remember who, "You know, we got a bunch of individuals on this team. We got white guys with pierced ears and crazy-lookin' haircuts. [Who, me?] We got farm boys. We got black guys with pierced ears. We got black guys with no pierced ears. We got everything. We're like one of those Long Island Iced Teas: all kinds of liquor mixed into one drink, and we'll *mess you up*."

That was one thing I liked about Switzer. He believed in people. He believed you could be whatever you wanted to be. He was an individual with a lot of strengths and a lot of weaknesses, a lot of lovable traits and a lot of terrible traits. But he was a human being and he wanted everybody else, all these young men, to try to find out exactly who they were too.

Why can't parents be like that? You don't know how many letters I get from kids asking me to help explain to their parents why they want to wear their hair a certain way. Their parents won't let them, even though they're not druggies or stoneheads or flunking out in school. How stupid is that? To me, the most ignorant thing a parent can do is blow up at his kid over a haircut. What if the kid was Mozart? Would he scream at him for the way he wore his wig? Or George Washington? Or John Lennon?

If your kid is different, why tear him apart? Be glad he's himself; he's an individual. Be glad he thinks for himself. If you jump his case, you're putting a strain on your relationship with your kid that you might not even realize. And it seems to me that you need to leave doors open for stuff that comes up later that really is serious.

Let the kid have fun. Before you know it, your kid will be gone. Eighteen comes faster than you think. And that's when he might show up on your doorstep with a dang burr cut.

CHAPTER 3

Football by Bozmosis

Like I said, I knew my life was going to change, for better or worse, the minute we won the national championship. One worse way is that people started seeing me as everything (a rebel, a punk, a jerk, a hero) except what I was at heart (a football player). Football is what I love to do more than anything—more than drink beers or spit on red tape or cause ulcers. I mean, without football, I might as well be a corpse somewhere with a tag on my toe. I was built to play the game.

Football gives me The High that nothing else does anymore. Like when you hit a guy so hard that his family feels it. That's The High. Or when they carry a guy off who's just been knocked out cold by yours truly. That's The High. I have a physical *need* to hurt people. I like the opposing sideline to go through more smelling salts the week they play me than they will the entire rest of the season. I ought to endorse smelling salts. "Hi. This is Brian Bosworth. When the last thing you see in your facemask is me, then you need . . . Acme Smelling Salts. At fine stores everywhere."

I've been around the world. I've ridden in the nicest cars, the most luxurious limos. I've stayed in the penthouse suite at the Trump Tower, been to a world heavyweight championship fight, been on magazine covers, and met some of the most famous people in the world. I've eaten at five-star restaurants and worn the fanciest clothes, but nothing does it for me anymore like football. Nothing gives me that High except football. That rush. I think I'd be dead without it. I'd be like Madonna without her batteries.

For me, football is more than a game or a sport or a job. For me, it's my whole ego on the line, my whole way of life. It's personal. When I'm lining up against somebody I hate, like John Elway of the Denver Broncos, or somebody I respect but hate, like Herschel Walker of the Dallas Cowboys, it's like a poolroom fight. It's like they're saying, "I'm a better human being than you." All right, grab a cue and let's go.

When I'm on the field, I have two goals: (1) get in fights; and (2) hit people in the head. Not too complicated.

First, fights.

I know most people think football fights are kind of moronic: two guys swatting at each other in suits of armor, basically just breaking their own fingers. But I know ways to really get in some damage. I try to get my hands underneath the guy's facemask. If you can get in there, you're jazzed. Because when you do that, you can just start scratching stuff; pulling noses and gouging skin and trying to rip lips and stuff. And there's nothing he can do until somebody comes to save his ass, 'cause your hands are jammed in his face and your own arms are protecting yours.

I love a good throwdown. I remember against Colorado one time I got in the best punch of my life—on the field or off. I was in a fight with this guy and I was just trying to hit the guy's earhole and I missed and I hit him right under the chin. It felt so solid. The guy just kind of buckled. I looked up and there was a ref staring straight at my ass. He couldn't wait to throw the flag. I got a penalty on the play, but it was worth it. I sent that poor sap to Dreamland. Nighty-night.

But fighting isn't just something I do to be obnoxious. It's part of the way I win. It's part of my style. It's a strategy the whole team can use. You start a fight with somebody, it gets everybody on your team excited, gets everybody jacked up, wakes everybody up. That's why I always try to get in a fight as soon as I can every game.

It takes a while to convince your teammates to try it, but once you do, it's addictive. When I first got to Oklahoma, nobody got in any fights. Nobody was trying to intimidate. It's intimidating playing a team that's always fighting because you don't know what they're going to do next. So for a while, I was the only one getting in fights. And the coaches would always go, "Boz, we don't need that." And I'd say, "Oh yes we do."

Pretty soon the guys were copping the same attitude I had. One game, Sonny said to me, "Damn, I just wish somebody would do something so I could get in a fight." Guys were itching to get a good swell-up going. The problem was, a lot of them didn't know how to start one. Let Professor Boz instruct you.

There are some surefire tricks. Like, if the guy is down, take his helmet and bang it a bunch of times against the ground. Or maybe stick your finger in his earhole and jam it around. Or get your hand up inside his helmet and do some scratching. Or knee him in the gut or the groin. Or step on his hand and twist away. Or maybe you call him a damn no-account low-class blankety-blank who should get his ass off the field if he's gonna play like a girl. And as you're getting up, use his helmet as a crutch. That gets him aware of you. That lets him know that you simply don't like his ass.

Maybe he acts tough and wants to fight, but the next time he gets the ball he's going to run with just a little bit less intensity than he did before that. Or he's going to be looking for you instead of the guy he's supposed to be watching out for. Or if he does want to run just a little bit harder, somebody is going to get hurt and it sure as hell ain't gonna be me. What you're doing is setting the tempo for the rest of the game and the rest of the team. It's the domino effect.

That's one thing that pisses me off when people compare me to Dick Butkus. Butkus was a great player, but I don't play like Butkus. I play like myself. I don't think Butkus and I are alike. Butkus didn't go into a game trying to piss people off, trying to fight people like I do.

That, and knocking people's brains into their necks. I love to hit guys in the head. That's my trademark. It may not be the most effective way to bring a guy down, but it's the most effective way for them to soil their Fruit of the Looms. Bruce Collie from the San Francisco 49ers said I tackle too high after we played them in the preseason my first year. Well, Bruce Collie holds too damn much.

Everybody says I tackle too high, but I do it because I'm going for the head. Nobody likes to be hit in the head. I hate getting hit in the head. Nothing hurts worse. And the more something hurts, the farther out of your way you'll go to be sure it doesn't happen again. It's like if you get a bad shock from your toaster. You just have cereal from then on.

Depending on how much time I have, I get to the guy and just grab his head and twist. If I'm flying at twenty miles an hour, that's even better. The best tackles for me are when I get a flying hit with a forearm right against his earhole. I always go for the earhole. The head's the target, but the earhole is the bull's-eye. Anytime you hit the earhole, you're hitting the head sideways and that means you've got a chance to give the guy a pinched nerve—and that means he's got to go out. One down. Ten to go.

People ask me if I feel bad when a guy leaves the game because of me. Like I'm supposed to have Merlin Olsen send the guy some roses. If I knock a guy out, I don't feel bad. You think he would feel bad if he knocked me out? We're not out on the field in all this equipment with all these people watching us so we can exchange addresses. Besides, I figure they'll be all right. I don't want to end their careers or anything.

Well, maybe there's one guy I'd like to wipe out for more than a game, maybe two or three games, and that's Elway. I can't stand Elway. The way he walks. That horse face of his. There's nothing about Elway I like. He doesn't even look athletic when he plays. He looks like a goofball.

But it doesn't matter who it is, I just want to do some damage. I guess it comes out of fear. My intensity comes from the fear of screwing up. Maybe that's because Dad was so hard to satisfy. Even if

we won, we'd go over the ways I messed up. We
wouldn't dwell on it, but I'd hear about it. So when
I'm out there, I just feel totally alone. I feel like I'm
out there all by myself and it's my job to make every
tackle. And I want to make every tackle a real jack;
one of those tackles that make you turn your eyes
away from the TV set.

I like hitting guys so hard that snot comes flying
out of their noses. I get a bigger rush out of just
knocking the crap out of somebody when they're just
totally dumbfounded as to what the hell hit them
than I do out of anything else in the world. I don't
mean tearing up somebody's knee; I'd never want
that. I'm just talking about knocking the living hell
out of them enough to where they have to go back
to the huddle and ask what city they're in. Or go to
the sideline and count their fingers. One thing I definitely want them to feel is that if they carry the ball
again, it's too soon.

Football is serious to me. No jacking around. I
may thrive on the show before the game, anything
to have a few laughs, but when I'm on the field, I'm
serious as a funeral. I'll hit anybody, anytime. Once,
in the final intra-squad game at the end of spring
ball in 1986, Jamelle threw an interception and then
just stood there, watching the guy return it on the
far side. I blindsided his ass, knocked him flying
into the sideline. I wasn't trying to hurt him. It was
a safe hit. But I was trying to teach him something.
I wanted him to know that there are maniacs out
there who think everybody is fair game. Like the
time Charles Martin of Green Bay wiped out Jim
McMahon's shoulder after that one interception. If
McMahon had learned the lesson I taught Jamelle,

he'd have forearmed Martin before anything could've happened.

I'll even wipe out a referee if I have to. And I have. I kind of like it. I'll catch them right in the middle of their stomachs. They just lie there for the longest time, trying to get their wind back, wondering why they didn't stay home and mow the lawn. It's not my fault. The rule book says they're part of the field. If a ref is in the way, I'm not going to go around him. "Pardon me, do you mind if I just get by you here so that I may bring Mr. Dickerson to a halt? Thanks kindly."

Refs can be useful too. I like to use them as a shield between me and blockers. If you get a referee in front of you and there's a blocker coming up on the inside of you, you just throw the referee into the blocker and then you can go around him. Or sometimes I'll just carry them along in front of me until I'm ready to make my move on a guy. Then I'll just push them down in front of the blockers so the blocker falls on top of his ass. Refs go down so easy. I'll yell at 'em, too, while I'm doing it. "Get the hell out of the way, old man, so I can run."

I like to heap a little abuse on them because they cause me a whole lot more grief than I cause them. Plenty of times they'll run into me and screw me up on a play. And I'm constantly yelling at them to get that damn flag out of their pocket and use it. Against Houston I got held up like I was a 7-Eleven and they never threw it.

The problem with yelling at refs is that you have to get up in their faces and that means you have to smell their breath. And they all have some serious halitosis because they sit there and drink all that coffee before the game. Haven't you ever wondered why you don't see players getting right up in an NFL ref's face, like they do in baseball? It's because they all have that serious hokeywolf breath, that real paint-peeling breath. They're all old mothers. I don't know if their breath is so bad because they're all just about to die or because they should've used the mint Polident instead of the regular. Got to get Pete working on this problem.

The whole NFL system of refs pisses the hell out of me anyway. I mean, here's big strong twenty-five- and twenty-six-year-old guys playing a money game—a *big* money game—and who do they send out there to decide it? Some sixty-year-old bluehair who can't even keep pace with the guys he's trying to officiate. I mean, these guys are insurance agents and accountants and bank vice presidents five days a week and then on weekends they get shipped all over the country to put on their costume and try to do a job. I mean, this is our profession. This isn't some goddamn hobby. This isn't the local Rotary Club weekly flag football league. How would they like it if once a week, say every Wednesday, some NFL players came into their bank and ruled on all their loans? "All right, throw this one out. Close this one. Give this guy all the money he wants. Okay, then, see you next week?" It doesn't make sense. Every other sport has full-time refs except the NFL. Another thing that pisses me off about refs is that they all want to talk to me before the game. I'm a curiosity to them. I'm like a sideshow. They want to meet me. "Hi, Boz! How are you today? Is that real paint in your hair? Yuck yuck." The old grandfatherly types will say that to me, the old raisin-headed creatures. But then when the game starts, they all of a sudden hate me. It's like they think I'm making too much money and they're all only making $28,000 a year refereeing and they're pissed. Or maybe they also don't like me because I bitch at them so much.

Like in the Green Bay game my rookie year, the guy tells me to take all my stuff off in the first quarter. I was pissed at Rozelle over his chickenshit handling of my number problem—I'll get to that later—and so I had tape on my shoes that said 44 BLUES and some other stuff as a protest. And now this ref is yelling at me to take it off.

I said, "You blind mother. You saw my ass before the game. Why didn't you tell me to take it off then? I'll tell you why. Because you wanted to make a spectacle out of me in front of seventy thousand people."

And on the next play I pushed his ass into a big pile of guys. I said, "Sorry, I didn't see you there in front of me." He never looked at me the rest of the day.

I guess it's no wonder I never get a holding call from the refs. I came to the sideline against Houston and I said to Keith Butler, my guru on the Seahawks, "Man, I never get the damn call."

And he said, "Of course you don't, you moron, and you never will."

"Why not?"

"Because it's *you*, you dumb shit."

Still, it's amazing to me what you can get away with when it comes to refs. They won't throw you out, no matter what you do. Because if a ref throws me out, say, in a game in Seattle, he might not work for a while. He's not going to throw people out because then our coaches would go to the league office and say, "We want him out. He's biased against us." And then where is he gonna work? Now he's got one less city to work in. And the Portland Breakers ain't here anymore, pal.

Refs are strange. You can call a ref every four-letter word in the language and finally, about the third quarter, he'll say, "Hey, watch it!" Don't know why they wait until then, but all of a sudden they'll say, "Watch it!" And I always say, "Well, somebody ought to, home boy, because you sure ain't, you sorry sack of prunes."

I also find it no problem to cheat in the NFL, partly because the refs are so old and crawling with barnacles. The best time is when the clock is winding down with less than two minutes to play. The ref doesn't have time to throw a flag on you because he's trying to spot the ball and the offense is in a real hurry. That's a great time, if you're in a pile, to twist somebody's head or put your finger in his ear-hole and try to rearrange his hearing. That *hurts* too. And there is nothing the guy can do about it. He can't holler or anything because he's facing the ground, grazing on turf. He's got some serious turf nose.

It was even easier to abuse guys in college because who would fight you? You could be dirty as hell and there wasn't anybody that was going to jump up and start fighting you. I mean, on our defense, you couldn't pick out one guy out of eleven you thought you could whip.

I guess if you could see what I'm like before the game—even two days before the game—you'd understand why I'm like what I am on the field. I'll admit it, I'm a complete asshole to be around, starting two or three days before the game. I'm ornery. Don't come near me. I don't even talk to people. I don't want to talk to people. In Seattle I just won't go out because if I do, someone will want to talk to me and I'll just feel like smashing them in the mouth and I just might. A perfectly nice person could come up to me the night before the game and I might put a hole in their head where no hole ought to be. I hate myself when I'm like that, but that's the way it is. Even my friends stay away. I figure there's time to party after the season's over.

Maybe it's because I cut off sex on Friday for a Sunday game. Maybe that's what makes me so adorable before a game. I get so uptight I can't sleep. I just lie there, thinking about the game. I also can't sleep the night before a game because of this ridiculous tradition in football of having *the home team* sleep in a hotel the night before the game. We did it at Oklahoma and we do it with the Seahawks. I mean, what's the point of having a home game if you're going to pretend you're on the road the night before? You're eating that death hotel food and sleeping on those torture chamber hotel beds and people are calling you, trying to get you to come down and sign autographs. I mean, I don't know how it happens, but they always find my room number and come knocking on my door. How am I supposed to sleep?

I guess the Seahawks do it because they think otherwise we'd be out drinking and partying until three in the morning before the game. I wouldn't be. Although, come to think of it, I know a lot of the guys on the team who would.

Anyway, as soon as I wake up on the day of the game, I'm gone, back to my house, to take a shower and go through my routine. Everything's got to be *exactly right* or I have to start over. Nobody's more superstitious than me.

I don't eat a thing on game days. By game time I want my stomach to be growling so loud you can hear it outside the stadium. I want my stomach to be tied in a thousand knots. That makes me want to beat the hemoglobin out of somebody even more.

I drive to the park and get hassled by fans coming out of my car going to the locker room. I don't sign autographs on game day. I don't have the patience. The mood I'm in, I might end up braining some kid, so I don't. I get a lot of abuse about it. I don't know why the Seahawks won't let me park someplace else, someplace closer to the locker room door, or get some security for me out there or something, but they don't. I have to make a dead sprint 150 yards from my car to the locker room door. The Seahawks have never had anybody like me there before. I know they'd admit *that*. But they've never had anybody who gets mobbed the way I do. I think they're starting to realize they've got to do something.

Once inside I do things the same way every time. It never varies. I always take eight concentrated caffeine pills. They're called Uptime. Each one gives you as much caffeine as four cups of coffee. So, if you count that, plus the two more I take at halftime, plus the one cup of coffee I drink when I first walk in, that's forty-one cups of coffee in one day. By game time I feel like Mrs. Olsen on a binge.

Then I take some kind of elixir, I don't even know the name of it. I don't even know what's in it. All I know is the stuff tastes awful. It tastes like water that has been fermenting for a month in a jar full of dirty jocks. It's just nasty. It's supposed to help with cramps. And I cramp up a lot because I go so hard. I remember at the Miami game my junior year, I was cramping so bad they filled me full of three IV bottles of sucrose solution at halftime and six more afterward.

So then I take four Advils for the headache I'm fixing to get from hitting people. It also loosens up some of the tendons I have. If I don't take it, I'll get a headache that feels like it's going to bust my skull open.

I don't take any uppers or drugs before a game. I don't know if anybody else does. I don't even look at anybody else. I'm lost in my own world. But I would never put that stuff in my body. I want to live past the age of thirty-two.

Then I get taped. Has to be the same way, same order every time, or we have to start over. Right foot, left foot. Right wrist, left wrist. Then the knees. I'm amazed how few people in the pros tape their knees. I never get on the field without my knee braces on. I've never missed a game—college or pro—in four seasons, so I must be doing something right. (Knock on wood).

Then I tear off ten pieces of tape, one for every finger. Otherwise, the pressure of some of the hits I give and get will cause the skin to split wide open. I like pain, but not that much.

So now it's just a few minutes before the game

and you've got a bunch of people, some of them players, trying to cheerlead to get people pumped up. To me, that's like giving a truckload of ice to an Eskimo. I've had thirty-three cups of coffee and I've been thinking about this game constantly for the last seven days. I don't need anybody pumping me up. If anybody tried to give me "The Gipper" speech or something, I'd probably rip their head off their neck. I'm like a rocket waiting to go off. Touch me from behind and you'd have to scrape me off the ceiling with a blowtorch.

I don't even know if we get a pregame speech or not because I'm just too out of it. I usually go into the bathroom and stare into the mirror. Sort of like: "You better be able to look yourself in this mirror when the game's over." Then everybody goes to a team prayer and I say my prayer at my locker by myself. Just a little talk with God.

I guess I get kind of involved in that because it seems like every time I'm the last one out the door. Some coach is usually screaming at me, "Come on! Let's go! Jesus, they're calling you! They're calling your name!" I hate to be introduced too. Just hate it. I'm always petrified that I'll trip on a crease in the carpet and blow out all over the place in front of all those people. Switzer did that once at an Oklahoma State game in front of a national TV audience. Caught a little seam in the carpet and—splat!—went down.

Once I'm on the field I feel totally useless until I've hit somebody hard. I try to make every hit as destructive as I possibly can. I try to set my tempo for myself, not for the other guys.

After the game I look forward to limping to the car. I look forward to waking up sore too. If I don't, that means I've wasted a week. If I'm limping, that means I left everything I had on the field. It gives me a sense of accomplishment, like a warrior. Like I've done something worthwhile with my life that week. I'm sore for three or four days, sometimes all the way up to the next game. The injuries hang on and hang on. The leg injuries, especially. I know by the time I'm thirty-five I'll be in some serious bad shape. I'll look like George Burns. I mean, right now I need help taking my shirt on and off, so I can imagine what's going to happen when I'm thirty-five. My knees hurt on cold days. I've got chunks of skin missing everywhere, one right near the top of my forehead. It's like somebody just took their finger and dug out a little hole for themselves. And I don't even know how or when it happened.

After the game I just want to be alone. I don't like to talk to anybody. I do my bit with the reporters and then shut up. I'm in my own little translucent world again. I can see out, but nobody can see in. I don't want any kind of conversation with anybody because they'll want to talk about the game and for some reason I don't want to talk about the game. I don't want to hear about it. I guess I think it's over and that's it. Nothing can be done and nothing can be said. Talk sort of cheapens it.

Of course, I'm wired on enough coffee to keep Toledo up for a week, so I just lie in bed the whole night, wide awake, thinking about the game. And, of course, I don't think about the good stuff. All I can think about are all the bad things that happened.

I won't be satisfied until I play a perfect game. And that's almost an impossibility. In three years at Oklahoma, I never even felt like I played a *decent* game. I'm never satisfied. That's probably from my father too. If I ever do play the perfect game, then I guess I'll have to quit.

Wouldn't the refs love that?

CHAPTER 4

Pranks for the Memories

One of the first skills I learned as an up-and-coming football player in my early teens was target vomiting.

This was back in high school, and when I think back on it, I can't believe it, but it happened, so I might as well 'fess up. Before our games we used to go to this all-you-can-eat-place, Duff's. We'd sit there and stuff our face with food you just don't eat before a game: greasy chicken and mashed potatoes, milk and bread and ice cream. We'd just gorge ourselves—all for $3.29. Now, stuffing yourself with that junk is the worst thing you can do before a game. Nowadays I won't eat before a game. Most guys that do only eat something a long time before the game, and then not very much. But we didn't know any better.

By the time the game started you'd start to warm up on the field and you'd start to feel queasy. By the first quarter you're working up a little sweat so you start drinking a lot of water. All that greasy food and all that water and all that running around, hitting people, was not a happy combination.

By the second quarter you'd be barfing between plays. You'd be fine and then all of a sudden you'd just have to blow. You'd try to do it right before the play. But one time I let it go right on a guy. He was sort of, well, *surprised* by it.

After that I trained myself to hold it in so I could barf on a guy after he was down. Totally sick him out. He'd get up with a horrified look on his face.

"What the bleep is wrong with you?" he'd say.

"I don't feel good," I'd say.

Even I'll admit that's gross. But the worst part is that we'd get on the bus home without taking a shower. And then we'd sit in the back of the bus and have our friends hand us a case of beer through the window from their truck as we were driving. The coach would never notice. He was always too pissed because we always lost. We won eleven games in my three years there and we had a lot more talent than that. So there we'd be, lying around the back of the bus, stinking from sweat and vomit, and sucking down beers as fast as we could drink them. You think that's what Springsteen had in mind when he wrote "Glory Days"?

My mom once told a reporter, "I'm glad Brian was the third child—or he'd have been the only one." And the worst part of that quote is that it's probably true. Everybody tells me I was a terror as a kid and I guess I still am. But, hey, it's in my blood.

I suppose she figured out I was going to be sort of a problem child when I was seventeen months old and I ripped the hinges off my crib. Maybe I was protesting the food or something. Or maybe it was when I was two and I disappeared from our house in Irving. When they found me, I was racing my tricycle down the middle of the Belt Line Parkway: SPEED LIMIT 45.

Or maybe it was when I was in the third grade. I

used to go visit my grandparents' ranch in Oklahoma. They had this humongous pine tree in the back and I used to climb it. One time I was pretending to be a fireman and slid down the thing without a shirt on. Most of the skin from my chest and my stomach stayed on the tree. My grandma said I had a little gleam in my eye, but that I never cried. Never let 'em see you sweat, right? Besides, how could I cry? My grandpa was every bit as tough as my father. He'd have said, "What the hell are *you* crying about?"

My mom says that it was at that point they believed I was totally immune to pain. That's not true. I just like to kick pain's ass.

Or maybe it was later, when the rebel in me started to come out. God knows I'd have hated to live in my neighborhood with me and my friends in it. I liked to think of myself as sort of a mini-Randall Patrick McMurphy, the character Jack Nicholson played in *One Flew Over the Cuckoo's Nest*. That's my favorite role in my favorite movie. I sort of modeled my philosophy of life after him.

Don't worry. God has paid me back for all the hell I raised as a kid. Somehow, no matter where I live, kids find out where it is and pull all kinds of stunts on me, mostly knocking on the door and running away at all hours of the night or doing stuff to my car or stealing my personalized THE BOZ license plates. I've been paid back a hundred times over. Not that I didn't deserve it.

I'd probably be dead or in jail or both if it wasn't for sports. At least that tired me out a little every day. My dad had me into every sport he could find by the time I was six and he was my coach for all of it. My dad played football in the service—linebacker and full-back. He was about 220 pounds in his prime and mean as a drill sergeant.

He had it kind of rough growing up. His father was an alcoholic. On the rare occasions he was home, he used to beat my dad a lot for no real reason. And later, when my dad got big enough, they used to beat *each other* up. But most of the time his father wasn't around at all. He was always out attending regular classes at the University of Jack Daniel's. My dad didn't have anybody to discipline him, nobody to correct him, show him how to do it right. And more than that, I guess, my dad didn't have anybody around to be proud of him.

That's why I think my dad worked me so hard. He wanted me to have someone to make proud, someone to achieve for. And that's a big reason why I didn't want to disappoint him. So that was one thing that made us close.

Dad just wanted me to be the best. He was always trying to get me to do better than the other kids. Like I said, sometimes first wasn't good enough. He taught me there's a difference between being first and being the best. You can be first and still not be the best. You can even be the best and know you didn't *do* your best. He knew what my ability was. He was looking past winning the junior high school softball throw or whatever it was. If he ever praised me, he didn't dwell on it much. But he didn't dwell on the bad parts either. "Oh, by the way, you stunk tonight."

"Thanks."

And I'm grateful he did. He drove me to this level. Sometimes my mom thought he was too hard on me.

Sometimes I did, too, I guess. My mom always thought I was doing as good as any other nine- or ten-year-old and she'd get on my dad's case about pushing me so hard. But he had his reasons. If I loafed, he'd make me run laps. The other kids would've gone home a long time ago and I'd still be running laps. Sometimes I think I still hear his voice in my head. "Don't loaf or Dad's going to be after your ass."

He started me out in the Pop Warner Football League, and I loved it right off. I played linebacker from the very beginning. But I was always a little smaller than the other kids and so he had all these schemes to get me bigger. He used to buy me all kinds of food. Used to get up every morning and fix me breakfast. "Get up, man, your breakfast is ready!"

"Don't want any. Gonna sleep."

"Get your ass up. I made a peanut butter shake for you too."

Wonderful. Nothing better than a peanut butter shake for breakfast. He'd always be making me a shake at the strangest times of the day. "Hey, want a shake? I'll make it! And how about a sandwich too?"

"Dad, it's eight A.M., Sunday morning."

They really went overboard trying to get me big and I don't think it was because I was first chair tuba in junior high. Whatever their reason was, they'd buy me special food at the grocery store and put it in the fridge with my name on it. And then, when my two sisters—Robbie and Vickie, both older—would ask for something, they'd get shot down.

And, of course, I was possibly the worst little

brother in the history of mankind. When my parents were gone, I'd chase my sisters around the house with my dad's bullwhip. They'd get these huge red welts. I'd just laugh. I'd use that whip whenever I wanted something. They wouldn't get off the phone or they'd try to change the TV channel or they'd eat my food. *Snap*. The whip. If my sisters are reading, I'd like to apologize to them now in front of the whole world. I was the worst. Forty lashes.

But if I dished it out at home, I took it at school. I was always in fights when I was a kid. Seems like from the third through the seventh grade, everybody wanted to fight me. One time twenty guys wanted to fight me in eighth grade. Good thing I was fast. Sometimes even my best friends would kick my ass. And if those guys weren't beating my butt, the principal was. At my school they could whack you—no problem. And it seems like every day I'd be in The Office, with the principal getting the board down off the wall and about to give me my licks for the day. Then my parents would hear about it and I'd get it at home, too, from my mom bearing a Hot Wheels track and from my dad with whatever he could find. My butt got beat more often than Columbia's.

I kept getting in hot water, even when I was too big to spank. It's amazing I could get in so much trouble in Irving. It was a dry town, so you couldn't get any liquor, and it never seemed like much happened. The highlight of the summers was going rat hunting with my twelve-gauge out in Hackberry Field. Too bad it's not kosher to hang rat heads on your wall because I got some beauties.

Most of the trouble I'd get in wasn't my fault. Honest. Whenever I'd do something at all, people would tell on me. I got suspended from high school for three days once for a food fight, it's true, but the whole cafeteria was on it. Okay, so I started it.

They were serving this Texas goulash, which really pissed me off. If you had ever had it, you wouldn't want it again. It was made of some kind of meat (I'm not sure from what animal), some macaroni, some tomatoes (I have no idea what country these tomatoes were grown in), and some multicolored junk. And it was all sitting in a big pile of grease, served up by hags in hair nets. I just didn't feel like eating it. I felt like throwing it. I was a junior, so I decided to throw it at the senior table. I threw it right at John Sullivan, a football player. Hit him right in the schnozz. Why? Because it was Texas goulash, that's why.

Now, once somebody sees somebody else coming up with something better to do with Texas goulash than eat it, the idea catches on. And pretty soon the whole cafeteria was slinging Texas goulash everywhere. Me and John slipped under the table by this time to get out of the firing line, but everybody else was into it. Welcome to goulash wrestling. The principal came running in there and right away all these goulash-covered people point to me.

I got 'em back, though. That summer I worked at this fast-food hamburger place—you'd know the name. And I used to do some horrendous things to people's hamburgers, just to break up the boredom. Like, I'd leave the paper on the hamburger meat when I'd cook it. That was tasty. Or I'd dip the meat in the jalapeño juice and then cook it. (Actually, some people liked that.) If I didn't like the person much, I'd rub his hamburger patty along the floor with my shoe before I'd cook it. If I *hated* the person, I'd put a bug right in the middle of the hamburger after it was done, then add ketchup and mustard and the buns and send it out. Then I'd sit there and watch the guy eat it. Sometimes, just before he'd bite into the middle, I'd say, "Wait a minute . . ." But sometimes I wouldn't, depending on the mood I was in. I'm pretty sure it was stuff like that which kept me from being Employee of the Month.

I had a sort of fondness for motorized vehicles and they always got me in the wringer. I snuck my mom's Z-28 out of the garage once and destroyed it. I wasn't even old enough to drive. I was going down the street next to my high school at about a hundred miles an hour when somebody decided he wanted to change lanes. I wrecked the car, but I almost killed my buddy Darrell. He was hanging out the window when the car changed lanes and he almost went flying out. By the time we crashed he probably wished he had.

I had a truck when I was fifteen years old, even though in Texas you don't get your license until you're sixteen. It was what you'd call a fixer upper. It didn't have a bed on the back, just a cab going down the street, and no lights or anything. I put a whole ton of illegal miles on that thing. I'd take it out late at night and drive it all over. I probably drove it more on people's lawns than on streets. It had this big strobe light on it, and we'd go out trying to find kids drinking beer illegally. We'd sneak up on them without the lights on and then all of a sudden—*zap!*—blind them with this huge searchlight. They usually thought it was the cops. They couldn't see who it was. And I'd say, in my loudest voice . . .

"All right, you kids! Just leave the beer where it is and get your asses on home or I'm taking you all downtown!" And—*bam*—they'd be gone in a flash. Best way in the world to get free beer.

Later on I had this motorcycle and a lot of times I'd ride around with two girls on the back. I always felt like causing trouble in that motorcycle. One time this lady was working on her lawn and there was this huge puddle in the middle of it. I saw her working next to that puddle and I just couldn't resist. So I took off as fast as I could and cruised right through that puddle and flooded that poor old lady. It was like a tidal wave hitting her. But I respected her. When I looked back, she was holding her rake in one hand and flipping me the finger with the other. I hope I'm still like that when I'm half-dead.

I'm not sure what makes me love pissing people off so much, but I always have. Maybe it was because I was born in 1965 and grew up in the 1970s, the most boring decade of the twentieth century. I was always bored. I needed stimulation. People at that time were comfortable. They were very comfortable. There were no protests, no social change. Everybody was just sort of standing pat, listening to K.C. and the Sunshine Band and painting everything lime green. My parents were pretty conservative too. Sort of a Texas version of "The Donna Reed Show." Maybe that suburban life drove me to want something completely different. Made me want to turn the whole thing upside down.

Not that I didn't get caught up in the mindless stuff myself sometimes. I was possibly the worst video junkie in Irving. One time, on one quarter, I played Defender for eight hours straight. I got more than 1.6 million points on it. I finally let myself get killed because my hands were cramping so bad. If I had spent as much time on the tuba as I did on video games, I'd be in the New York Philharmonic, making $23,000 a year.

I'll bet over the years I've spent a solid year of my life staring at video games. I've probably spent $5,000 in quarters too. Playing video games on the road is one of the only places people will leave you alone. "Sorry, I can't sign your baby's bib right now. Playing Donkey Kong." For some reason, people will respect that. But they'll take a fork out of your mouth at a restaurant.

I wasn't a total degenerate in high school. A lot of times I'd go to keg parties and I'd bring my own milk because I was trying to take care of my body. And I stayed out of the gang fights in town—Irving High vs. MacArthur High. You think of gang fights as being in L.A. and Chicago, but we had them. Anytime you mix rich kids with poor kids and tough street kids with suburb kids, you're going to get fights. I'd be around, but as soon as they started bringing out the guns and chains and knives, I was gone.

Without sports, though, I might have jumped right in. I always had some practice to go to. I wasn't bad at basketball, in fact. I averaged twenty-four points a game as a freshman on the sophomore team. I could one-hand dunk it too. I'm still good enough that the black guys on the team will let me play with them. But my sophomore year, the head basketball coach was an asshole and decided to put me on the varsity. That team had seven seniors on it. He knew I'd sit the whole year, but he didn't care. So I got bored. So instead of working at basketball, I spent all my time in the weight room. All of a sudden I was getting bigger—going from 165 to 180—and that's when I decided to concentrate on football.

I played quarterback and linebacker as a freshman. I was smooth as brown sugar on that veer offense, don't you know. But I hated offense even then. I really hated playing quarterback. You stand there, you're carrying the ball, and everybody's got a free shot at you. Most of the guys don't clip their fingernails, so they're scraping the hell out of your neck when you run by. I played tight end and linebacker the next year on the varsity and that was a little better. At least at tight end you got to block down on a guy who didn't know it was coming; wipe them out from the side. But still, you were going to hit sooner or later. Forget that. I knew defense had the better deal. In defense, you're the forearmer, not the forearmee.

But believe it or not, as bad as we were and as many stupid things that we did, I was getting better and better as a player. I was strong and I never missed a game. It's something my dad taught me. He had a rule that I could *never* come out of a game. He said that people were depending on me to do a job, that I'd committed to do it and I was going to do it. He said I wasn't going to be a quitter. Said if I quit people would stop counting on me. So I played with twisted ankles and bruised thighs and jammed fingers and everything. One time, when I was nine, I ripped my thumbnail off during a game and didn't tell anybody because I didn't want to come out. If I

sprained my ankle, we'd just tape it up tighter and
I'd try to block it out of my mind. I just kept telling
myself, "I'm not going to be a pussy and quit now."
I've never missed a college game or a pro game yet,
so maybe that's where I got it. I know there've been
a few times when I damn sure felt like staying out.

So I had a reputation for being tough and for being
a hitter and, as it turned out, I had damn good speed.
I've been timed in a 4.59 forty-yard dash, which is
as fast as most running backs. I haven't run into a
running back yet—except for Bo Jackson—who can
beat me to the outside.

I knew I was going to be good, even though my
coach, Ronnie Cox, didn't think so. Get this. He
comes up to me with two games left in my senior
season and he says, "Brian, if you really play well
these last two games, there's a chance I can get a
couple of junior college coaches to take a look at
you."

That blew my mind. Here I was: my dad and I
had been setting up official recruiting trips all over
the country to some of the biggest-name schools in
college football—Oklahoma, Texas A & M, Texas
Tech, LSU—and this nimrod is trying to get me a
junior college scholarship. I just said, "Thanks a
lot." The guy was too far gone to throw him a clue
line.

I wasn't sure any of the papers knew what they
were talking about either. Some big-deal recruiting
ratings guy named Max Emfinger, out of Houston,
didn't even rate me as a linebacker. He put me at
defensive end and even then he only put me in his
top three hundred list. Somebody ought to find Max
Emfinger and rip his typewriter away from him. The

Omaha *World-Herald*'s blue-chip report didn't even have me on its list of about one hundred linebackers and defensive ends.

I didn't give a damn if the papers didn't think I could play; the coaches did. Switzer came to my house a bunch of times, four or five. He exceeded the number of official visits he was supposed to make (three), but then, so did every other head coach who visited me. Switzer was the best, though. He'd come to my high school during the lunch hour—when the most possible kids could see him—wearing his big fur coat, walking down the hall with his arm around me. I thought he was cool as hell.

SMU supporters and alumni, just like you'd figure, were the most blatantly criminal. They tried everything. I'd get phone calls every night from people in Dallas, saying, "Hey, we really want you at SMU. Don't worry about anything. We'll take care of everything. Get you a place to live. I got some buddies that own some condos. And don't worry about transportation. I got a buddy who owns a dealership. And I'm sure you'll need some clothes to fit in at a school as nice as SMU, so we'll set you up with a nice wardrobe. If you need to go out and buy stuff, we'll buy your game tickets and anything else you have."

They just flat-out told me everything that they eventually got busted for. When I heard that pitch, I realized they were fixing to go on probation. I didn't want to be sitting on some team that can't play on TV and can't go to a bowl for ninety-nine years. Besides, their coach Bobby Collins, I wouldn't trust as far as I could spit.

A long time later, when I ended up signing with

Oklahoma, my mom started getting all these threatening calls from SMU types. ''Mrs. Bosworth? I hope your son likes it at Oklahoma because we'll make sure he never gets a job in Dallas. He'll never accomplish anything in Texas again.'' Nice to see the SMU alumni understand it's just a game.

Some places I went were unreal. At Tech I showed up and they've got a limousine and a girl waiting for me. They don't say it, but it's pretty obvious you could have the girl right then and there and you wouldn't have to feel bad about not calling her the next day, if you know what I mean. A lot of the hostesses I met might just as well have worn a lapel button that said: HI! I'M WHORING FOR GOOD OL' STATE U. But what the hell. That's Texas. I didn't want any of that stuff anyway. I wasn't going to choose a school because they could get me laid. I could do that on my own. I was more interested in finding a school that wanted to win.

At LSU they wanted to give me the authentic tour, I guess, so they took me to a Cajun restaurant. I got sick as a dog from it. I drank bottles of Pepto-Bismol for a week after that.

I had a great time at A & M. They set me up with anything I wanted. The guys there were terrific.

Notre Dame recruited me as a tight end, if you can believe that. But I looked at the roster and saw that all their tight ends were six-four and six-five and Polish, so I said forget it. No way you beat out a six-five tight end named Novotny.

Eventually, it all came down to A & M and Oklahoma, and I guess in the back of my mind, I knew that was no contest. I was born in Oklahoma City. My parents met at OU. My dad worked at Tinker

Air Force Base. We moved to Dallas after that, but I grew up following Oklahoma football. My dream was to become the greatest Oklahoma linebacker of all time. I remember saying before my first game in 1984 that by the time I left, I hoped people would talk about me the way they do Shoate and Cumby. No way I was going anywhere else.

Besides, the first time I walked into Owen Field in Norman, I got goose bumps the size of golf balls. I was awed by it the first time I saw it and most every time I walked into it after that. You see all those national championships on the scoreboard. They've got that Hall of Fame. They've got the All Big Eight players on the wall inside the locker room. And when I saw the weight room, I was hooked. It was only about the size of Rhode Island.

As soon as I came home from that trip, I knew I was going to be a football player for the University of Oklahoma.

Good thing I had no idea what that meant.

CHAPTER
5

Life Without Rules

The first time I knew I'd really like the University of Oklahoma was the day running back Buster Rhymes opened up his balcony door at the Bud Wilkerson Athletic Dorm and fired about a hundred and fifty rounds out of an Uzi machine gun.

Buster was from Miami and he hated snow. It was a tradition in Norman after the first snowfall to have a humongous snowball fight. I guess Buster didn't like snowball fights either. And he definitely didn't approve of people throwing snow at *him*. He was walking along, minding his own business, and somebody hit him with a snowball. He got a little upset. So right in the middle of the fight, Buster went up to his room, opened his door, and let fly with this Uzi above all their heads. Just a few innocent warning blasts. Just like the kids at the University of Beirut get now and then. I have no idea where he got the Uzi, except that everybody I knew from Miami seemed to have no trouble coming up with stuff like that. That dispersed the snowball fight pretty quick and I can't recall anybody throwing a snowball at Buster Rhymes after that.

Of course, we had a team meeting afterward about it. The King, Barry Switzer, our head coach, was *pissed*. But not too pissed, I guess, because nobody got thrown in jail over it. Switzer was smart. He'd give up his fur coat before he'd lose a player over something stupid.

I was only a redshirt freshman, but I learned a lesson from that. If you were a star on the University of Oklahoma football team, you could do just about anything you wanted. You had no rules. If the King wanted you playing Saturday, you played, no matter what you did Friday night. Anybody remember the last time Switzer suspended somebody good from the Sooners team if he had a choice in the matter? Hard to believe anybody did anything wrong in his fifteen years there, I know, but you'd think somebody might've been caught doing *something*.

But that was fine by me. The Oklahoma football team makes the university $10 million a year and the players don't get a dime for it. It's slave labor. It's un-American. "Here, boys, room and board. If you want to go out and get a pizza or see a movie, you're on your own." So whatever we were allowed to get away with was fine by me. And I admit, I tried everything. And got away with most of it.

I got everything and anything I wanted in Norman. I can hardly remember paying for a thing. My meals were almost always free. Everyplace I went, they'd say, "Oh yeah, let me take care of that for you." So many people picked up my checks in restaurants that it got to the point that if the waitress handed me the check, I'd say, "What the hell am I supposed to do with this?" And I'd go up to the manager and say, "You gonna take care of this or what? You don't expect *us* to pay for this, do you?" I guess you could say I got spoiled.

But you *had* to eat out because the OU food was

so horrible. They'd give you frozen steaks, which weren't so bad, I guess, except that the damn things were still frozen when you ate them. They'd be charred black on the outside and frozen inside. We'd yell at the poor cooks. It wasn't those ladies' fault, but we'd yell anyway. "Damn, we make this place ten million bucks a year! When are we gonna get some real goddamn food?"

So we were always going out to dinner. We had a ritual on Wednesdays called "Geno"—G.N.O., Guys' Night Out—and I must say, even by my standards, those were sick evenings. No women allowed. We'd go to this one place, Garfield's, and drink beer and just get stupid. They had this club called The Silver Bullet Club. To belong in it you had to drink a hundred beers there. When you did, you'd get your name on this plaque. We got in the club in about three Wednesdays—thirty-three beers a night. You can go in to this day and see our names.

There'd be about fifteen or twenty of us and we'd be in there all night. We'd eat dinner there. All the crabs and prime ribs you could eat, fifteen bucks. They'd always set the desserts on the table in front as you walked in, so people could see what they were, but on Wednesday nights that table was raped and pillaged. We'd take everything. One time some of the other guys had these water machine guns, battery-operated. The place was full of people. By the time we got through fighting with those things, there was nobody left in the joint. It's no wonder. Some guys got blotto drunk and took pistols into the bathroom, filled them full of piss, and started shooting the manager. I'd have hated to be his dry cleaner.

The coaches finally found out about all of this and

tried to put a stop to it because the defensive backs were screwing up or something. So the defensive backs stopped going. But we kept going. Somebody would say, "I'm not supposed to go there anymore." And I'd always say, "Can't go? What do you mean can't go? What are they going to do, bench you?" And we all knew the answer to that. If you were good enough, they wouldn't bench you, no matter what you did. Switzer wanted to win. Simple as that.

Switzer isn't a cheater. Switzer doesn't have a slush fund and doesn't set up payments to players or any of that. He's smarter than that. Switzer just turns his back and lets players fend for themselves. He never wanted to know how it was that I was living in a nice $500-a-month condo, watching a big-screen TV, driving a Jeep and a Corvette, and always operating with $2,000 in my checking account. And he never asked. Neither did our athletic director, Donnie Duncan, or our bonehead university president, Frank E. (for Error) Horton, higher learning's answer to *Beetlejuice*.

I mean, if you could've seen the athletic dorm parking lot at OU, you'd have thought there was a doctor's convention going on inside. And ours wasn't ever as ritzy as SMU's or A & M's or a lot of other schools. Most college football coaches are like the father of a girl who's just come in from a date. He'd rather not know the details, so he doesn't ask.

I never felt bad about the way I lived at OU, which was like a prince, because the money I made that place, the national publicity I brought it—all of which translates into more admission requests and more university donations—was more than anybody in the state could've done for it, including the governor or His Dishonor, Horton. A typical example was one time when I was a sophomore, I made a poster for the university showing me in this ROTC outfit, greasepaint on my face like I was a soldier, with a pointing stick in my hand, showing a map of all the places we were going to search out and destroy that year—Lincoln, Nebraska; Miami; Boulder, Colorado—stuff like that. And at the top it said MASTERS OF DEFENSE.

They sold hundreds of thousands of copies of that poster at five bucks a shot. Everywhere I went in the state of Oklahoma, I'd see that damn poster and I never got a nickel from it. And neither did the team. One time I went up and asked a lady in the OU souvenir shop on campus about it.

"Where does the money go from this poster?"

"Oh, it goes back into concessions," she said. "We buy more stuff to sell."

I said, "How many have you sold?"

"About a hundred and fifty thousand, I think."

This was about two months after it came out.

"A hundred and fifty thousand at five bucks a pop! That's about three quarters of a million dollars! That's a lot of sweatshirts and ashtrays! When is somebody gonna cut me a check out for all of this?"

She didn't know. And I'm still not totally convinced all that money went to buy concessions. I'm sure there's some bigwig at OU lying around his pool right now that I built for him. I mean, they made three quarters of a million dollars off that poster, yet if I accepted a quarter pounder with cheese from my coach, the school is busted. Now tell me the NCAA makes sense.

If an Olympic track athlete, somebody like Carl Lewis, does a poster, the money goes into a trust fund that "distributes" the cash to Lewis later. Here's the way they distribute it: "Okay, Carl, you get all of it. See you later." So what's the difference? He's getting the money flat-out. But Lewis gets to stay an amateur. He doesn't have anybody like the NCAA up his butt about it. I was an amateur, too, but it seems we had two different definitions going. Lewis gets the money for the use of his name and face and I get handshakes from assholes in suits and ties.

As important a fund-raiser as I was to Oklahoma, the NCAA—National Center for Aging Assholes—expected me to live on tuition (room and board), not take a job, not drive a car, not be able to take my girl to a movie, not buy a new shirt when I needed one, not buy an album if I felt like it. Meanwhile, every day I'm talking to the New York *Times* and Brent Musburger and *Sports Illustrated*, representing the University of Oklahoma. The way I looked at it, they should've let me stay in the president's house. They could've put his ass in the dorm.

That's what I mean when I say you're on your own. Anything I got at Oklahoma I got on my own. Switzer never set it up. Neither did the university. That's the way it is at most schools. The player is on his own to survive, to make the best deal he can. How else is he going to go to school, practice four hours a day, and attend meetings for another four? I mean, how stupid is it to think that a head coach can control the lives of eighty guys on his team, make sure nothing is given to them by alumni? Do you know how many alumni OU has? Do you know how many people who aren't alumni that want to see that you have a few extra bucks, still want to be "part of it"? Is it illegal to have somebody who wasn't an OU alumni give you something? How about a friend of a friend of somebody who went to OU? The NCAA is about as pertinent to the real world as tits to a motorcycle.

I had a guy—not an OU alumnus—who used to set me up. He was a professional businessman who was treating me well because he knew that someday I'd be making some serious money and he'd get my business. Just a straight business public relations move. What's wrong with that? He helped me buy my 'Vette. I got money from this guy for doing certain jobs. Like checking my mailbox once a week. It was his choice. Does the NCAA have power over businessmen?

There were other people—alumni, ex-players, fans, people in the town—who wanted to play the Godfather or something and I'd let them. They'd come up to you and they'd want you to like them. They figured if you liked them, they fit in. It made them cool, made them young again, I guess. Everybody was like that. OU was a winner, so they figured if they were part of it, they were winners too.

That made life in Norman a breeze for me. Everybody wanted to help. I don't know how many traffic tickets I got out of during college. Thirty? Forty? I didn't even have to come up with a good line for the cop. All I had to do was show my license and he'd let me go. "Uh," he'd say in some dumb voice. "I just wanted to wish you good luck this Saturday." He might as well let me go because if he wrote me a ticket, I'd just call my buddy in the district attorney's office in Norman and say, "Got a ticket."

"Okay, what's the number on it?"

And that would be it. He'd call the police station and say, "Okay, when the Boz's ticket comes in, lose it." Thank you very much.

I guess when you think about it, if I couldn't get a ticket, that meant I had no rules on the road. Having no rules is a great way to drive. You can pretty much break any laws you want. It's like *The Road Warrior*. Just try to survive. You can go through any lights you want. Color is no object. You can do whatever you want to the car in front of you, go over any lawn you like, and drive on all the shoulders you want to get by any traffic jam you desire. I did all of that and more. If it ever took me more than ten minutes to get anywhere in Norman, then I must not have had my heart in it.

Having no laws also means you can go as fast as you want—and I like to go very fast. One time I went 156 miles an hour in a Trans-Am coming home from a basketball game in Ringland, Oklahoma. This is where "diagonal driving" comes in handy. The definition of diagonal driving: when you've got twenty minutes to get to the airport and it's a forty-minute trip and you make it with five minutes to spare.

What diagonal driving is is firing your car as fast as you can as close as you can to the rear bumper of the car in front of you, then jerking your car into the next lane just in time, then back in front of the car you just passed as near to his bumper as you can. Unless he's Richard Petty, this freaks him out. Not only is it fun, but it scares the breakfast out of him.

The state of the art of diagonal driving right now is in Los Angeles, and I must admit I am a world-class diagonal driver there. In L.A. I'll rent a big old stinkin' Lincoln from Budget and be doing about eighty on the highway. Got to have something big in case you don't diagonal fast enough sometime. If you've been to L.A., you know how traffic can just come to a sudden stop, even in the fast lane. Well, the idea is not come to a stop. I've locked up those brakes and missed a bumper by an inch, then weaved into the shoulder, and then back into traffic. It tends to irritate people somewhat. You know how they had a bunch of shootings on L.A. freeways there for a while? Well, I'm afraid I might have instigated that.

I'd drive like that in Norman, too, but the cops didn't mind. They just wanted to be part of the program. Norman cops helped me out a lot. I remember one time these assholes from the military base nearby were waiting in a Camaro outside our practice field for some players to come out to give shit to. Me and Stevie Bryan and Dougan Forrest came out together. Dougan could see they wanted to fight, so he started screaming at them, but it didn't work. So we asked them to leave and they wouldn't.

So, this goes on for a while and I notice they've got a twelve-pack of beer in the back of the car. So I said, "Well, if we're going to stand around and argue, you won't mind if we have a few of your beers to quench our thirst." We started drinking their beer and they started getting upset.

All of a sudden this university police car pulls up. It's a big old fat guy, and he said he'd gotten a call that there was a disturbance in the parking lot.

"Yes, sir, Officer," I said. "There is a little bit

of a disturbance here. These boys here from the Air Force are drinking beer.'' I took my beer and set it inside the dash. ''And look, here's an open can of beer right here on top of the car.''

And the guy in the car starts squirming. ''Officer, we didn't drink that . . .''

''And there's a bunch more in the backseat, Officer,'' I added helpfully. To be even more helpful, I reached back there and I popped one open and said, ''See?''

The guy in the car tried to grab it from me and the cop said to the Air Force guy, ''You know you ain't 'sposed to have no open container in the car in the state of Oklahoma. What's wrong with you, son?''

''He just opened it right in front of your eyes,'' the guy said.

''Would it help him if the can was empty?'' I asked the officer.

''A little.''

So I poured it out all over the car.

Then the cop goes, ''Well, do you think there is going to be any more problems here, Brian?''

''No, sir, Officer. These gentlemen were just fixing to leave.''

And when he drove off, you should've seen the look on those guys' faces. We dragged them out of the car and had a serious smash-mouth session. Our smashes and their mouths. And just before they took off, a lot worse off than when they showed up, I managed to grab the rest of the twelve-pack out of the backseat.

I don't know why the cop helped us, except that everybody in Oklahoma wants to feel like they're contributing to the cause. They don't make a single tackle, but they think they're part of it then. So if they want to pick up your dinner check and feel big-time, who was I to stop them? If somebody wanted to pay for your clothes when you brought them up to the register and if that made them feel good, okay by me. I'd talk to them if I liked them or not talk to them if I didn't feel like it. I didn't owe anybody anything, except to play my ass off for them on Saturday.

As a matter of personal pride, I never let my bank account get below $2,000 in Oklahoma. I had my methods, a little more sophisticated than most guys. But I knew plenty of players at other schools and most of them did it by selling their season tickets. Here's how it worked at a certain school in Texas (not SMU, which never bothered covering it up).

Each player would get a certain number of season ticket books. Freshman got two, sophomores three, and so on. Depending on who you knew or how big a star you were, you could sell your book for between $80 and $400. But you'd always hold out the biggest game of the year for a bonus. Like, we heard that guys at Texas held out the OU–Texas ticket and got much as $250 for it, depending on how generous the guy was feeling, how much he wanted to see the old puke-orange-and-beige win. And if you could get your hands on a sideline pass, that would go for a good $400 to $500 for one game.

Of course, not everybody on a team knows the ropes of how to do it, or has the energy to do it. So some guys would go up to a freshman and say, "Look, I'll give you $100 for your book right now." Then they'd turn around and sell it for a cool $300 profit. If you did that with ten guys, that was $3,000 profit, plus whatever you made on your own. Junior Achievement.

Tell me what's wrong with that. How the hell else is a player supposed to get money? The morons at the NCAA won't let us work during the season, only during the summer. But the competition at the top level in college ball is so intense you've got to be training and lifting weights all summer if you want to be any good. The only time I worked was my first year. I couldn't afford to work the last three years or I'd have slipped as a player. College football is a year-round, full-time *job*, not some stamp-collecting hobby. You ever wonder why you never see any two-sport athletes anymore? It's amazing anybody can even get through school with the eight-hour days they want out of you. And the National Brain Deads in Kansas City want you to get a summer job bagging groceries at the local A & P. Right.

It's all such a scam, the summer job programs at the big schools. Of course, you might have heard about my summer job working the auto-assembly line at General Motors. I'll get to that later. But I've had some other jobs worth mentioning. One year my job was to go sit in my car and watch an oil rig go up and down for four hours. I'd make $100 a day for that. My job was to make sure nothing happened to that oil rig in that four hours. And let me say I was one of the premier oil-rig watchers in the country. Under my guidance, nothing ever happened to that oil rig.

People give you these jobs to contribute to the cause. Girls always seemed to want to contribute too. Personally, I had a girlfriend all through college, so I didn't mess around, but I saw enough stuff at our dorm to make a blue movie.

For some reason, sometimes a girl came to the dorm late at night who didn't feel like it was enough to contribute to just one guy. Lots of times, they'd contribute to a whole lot of guys. This is called "being true to your school." We called these girls freaks. I never messed with a freak because my girlfriend would've come at me with an icepick if she ever found out. But my roommates did and I'd always end up hearing about it.

I had this one teammate my freshman year who was just plain demented. We lived on the fourth floor and he liked to bring cats up there and throw them out the balcony door, just to see if they'd land on their feet. They would. Or he'd be too tired to make it to the bathroom two doors down, so he'd go out in the hall and piss in a corner. A defensive lineman. What a sick person he was. This guy was such a scam artist that he once convinced a girl that he was Englebert Humperdinck and he said he was spending a semester at OU as research for a movie he was going to do. Real brain surgeon, this girl.

Anyway, this guy was really sick. He'd get these freaks and he'd slambola on *my* bed. I'd be at my girlfriend's and he didn't want to wreck *his* sheets, so . . .

There was a tradition among some guys that if anybody got a girl to come up to their room, they had to inform the guys of it. Like one guy would say, "Got a babe coming to my room in thirty minutes," and next thing you know there'd be five guys jockeying for position in his closet. I know this sounds perverted. That might be because it was.

You'd get in there and you'd have to stuff a sock in your mouth to keep from laughing. We got caught a lot. Sometimes it was tough for the guy in bed because the guys would be banging around in the closet and making noise and the girl would look up and say, "What was that?"

"Uh, thin walls."

The funny thing was, the guys who were in charge of the dorm never thought anything funny was going on. There was this old guy in charge named Port Robinson, an old wrestling coach from a long, long time ago. I think he coached for the University of Socrates for a while. He was a great old guy, funny, but kind of out of it. And he had this thing that you couldn't have a TV in your room if you were a freshman. I guess he thought if you had a TV you wouldn't get anything done. But I was a 3.3 student and I took care of my studying when I had to and screwed around when I had to. So I'd sneak a TV in and hide it in the closet. I'd put a towel over it and put my shoes on top of it so it looked like a box. This is how ridiculous it was. I'd have to sneak into the closet to watch "Gilligan's Island" reruns. Yes, college is a real growing experience.

Port would come check the rooms and one time he came in and found a fire hydrant my roommate had stolen. God knows how he got a fire hydrant. I said at the time, "What the hell is that for?" He said, "Man, it looks good!" Port came in and saw the fire hydrant, which was sitting right next to the TV in my closet. So he looked under the towel and saw the TV. Any time Port found a TV, he put it in his storage room downstairs. So we snuck down there one night through the window, took our TVs, and then took another one, which we took down to the pawn shop and hocked. Port never missed any of 'em.

I loved to see what I could get away with at OU. My favorite thing was to get picked up at the Oklahoma City airport in a blue stretch limo. It was gorgeous. It had a VCR in the back and a TV, stereo, and wet bar. You could just stretch out in style. I'd get off the plane and there'd be my limo waiting. It was perfectly legal too. It was a friend of mine's business. He wasn't an OU graduate or anything. He did it for me for free and every now and then I'd recommend him to somebody else, some high roller in town I'd know, somebody who needed a limo. It was more than a profitable relationship. But if you asked the National Coneheads in Kansas about it, they'd bust a gasket. But I defy you to tell me how that's illegal.

And let's face it. School was no real chore. I don't know why, but I found it easy. School was a blowoff for me. I'd study as much as I had to to get an A or B and that wasn't much. There is nothing to school. And it's not like the professors would give you a break either. People think football players get a free ride through college, professors giving them the answers, letting them cruise by, changing grades. That's total bull. If anything, college football players get the raw end of the deal from professors.

To college professors football players are everything they hate. We get all the girls, get to travel, and don't have to care who's published the latest dissertation on fifteenth-century Olde English poetry. What really hacks them off is knowing that some of us will probably make ten times as much as they ever will. And they hate the line ''The OU football team wants a school it can be proud of" because they know it's really true. At OU the tail wags the dog. I mean, when was the last time you saw seventy-five thousand people pay twenty bucks on a Saturday afternoon to watch the debate team?

I had one professor who was a looney tune. I got a B on the paper and a B on the midterm, but he tried to drop me for nonattendance. I didn't attend much because the syllabus didn't say anything about attendance being required. The class was so simple all you had to do was read the textbook. I went in to complain about it and he said, "Have you ever met my daughter? She's about nineteen. She's going to start school here next year. Here's a picture of her. Would you like to call her?" Do you believe that? Ten seconds after the guy drops me for no reason, he's got the balls to try to set me up with his daughter!

But I managed. I took a full load every semester and more than a full load, eighteen credits, my last semester, just so I could graduate early. I went to college under the premise that I would graduate. I didn't want to go to college and come up six or ten years from now, saying, "Yeah, I went to college."

"Oh yeah? What's your degree in?"

"Uh, I don't know. Let me check."

Unfortunately, a whole lot of players in colleges aren't like that and the athletic departments aren't all that interested in changing their minds. The athletic departments want to keep them *eligible*, but graduation is another thing. Most guys took whatever courses had the easiest teachers or gave you the most credits for the least work. This means, of course, P.E.

Some players shouldn't have been in college at all. No way. They could barely read a stop sign. At OU, for instance, they would get them into these remedial classes, classes that tried to lay down the foundation for them to be able to take regular classes. They were going three steps backward to go one step forward. It's possible that they would've graduated, but it'd have taken eight or nine years. So they'd do what they could. I knew a guy at another school who took almost nothing but correspondence courses. All he had to do was write three papers for each class and the three papers were sitting in the football office files. All he had to do was copy the things and he passed. The guy's degree should've been in Advanced Xeroxing.

The whole reason most of my teammates were in college was to play the game. I knew it. They knew it. The coaches knew it. The teachers knew it. And if they weren't so good at coming up with square roots or discussing Keynesian economics, they sure as hell could play football.

Christ, could they play football.

CHAPTER
6

A Few Screws Loose

Happy was always something I was looking to be my first year in college. I had fun in the dorms, but I was redshirted, which means I didn't play the whole year but didn't lose a year of eligibility either. Not playing football was seriously flaring my hemorrhoids.

Basically, Switzer had held me out that year, 1984, because he didn't want me to be part of a screwed-up team. That was the year they went 7-4, Switzer's third straight four-loss season, and his job was in jeopardy. That was a selfish team, a lousy team to be on, and Switzer didn't want me or most of the guys in my class to be a part of it. They had a lot of guys that were real concerned with their stats, worrying if they were going to be named All-American or not. Guys like Jackie Shipp and Thomas Benson and Buster Rhymes—Mr. Uzi himself—guys whose main concern was what their contracts were going to be in the NFL.

Our class wanted no part of that bullshit. We had a bunch of young guys who wanted to come in and change things. No way we were going to have four-loss seasons. We didn't even want one-loss seasons. So none of the new guys hung with the seniors. We hated the seniors. We couldn't wait for them to leave so we could take over.

But as much as I didn't want to be part of that year, I didn't really want to redshirt either. I mean, that was the first year I'd sat out of anything in my whole life. Plus, my shoulder was hurt, so I didn't get to practice. That meant I had no competition that whole year. I remember that it made me crazy to watch the team play. I couldn't sit through an entire game. I knew that I could do a better job than the people who were in there. But more than that was the feeling that all of a sudden I was a nobody. Just another number.

But Switzer, in a class move, took everybody to Hawaii for the final game of the year and that's when he pulled me aside and told me something that really changed his relationship with me and changed my career at OU. He sat me down at a table and said, ''Look, I need you to play better than a freshman next year. I need you to play on a senior level. I need you to take charge. I need you to be the team leader.''

He couldn't have said anything better to me. Finally I had somebody counting on me. It was a big thrill for me, a great moment. I love a challenge. All of the new guys, the freshman and sophomores, sat down and decided we needed a goal. And we decided we wanted to bring the Big Eight championship back to Oklahoma, where it belonged. OU hadn't won it since 1980 and that was going to be our ultimate driving force for the year.

We didn't realize until much later how dumb that idea was.

I came out that spring like a madman. I wanted

to do well for myself and not let Switzer down. I wanted it so bad that I played that whole spring with a separated shoulder. I just couldn't bear to sit around anymore. One day in practice I took about five guys' helmets off in a row. One of the coaches told me later they were afraid that one of them would still have the head in it.

I won the starting job and I was ready to make my mark on OU football history that fall. But first I had to make my mark on General Motors history that summer. Not that I was trying to. They forced me to.

The first thing I want to point out is that I *like* GM cars. I've always driven Corvettes. In Seattle I got offered Mercedeses, Porsches, Lotuses, everything. But I chose a Corvette. That's got to count for something, right?

But they treated me unfairly, really unfairly, so I got them back. I simply told the truth about something and it caused all sorts of hell. I told *Sports Illustrated* that out of sheer boredom sometimes, some of us, including me, on the GM line in Oklahoma City would hang a screw or a bolt off a piece of thread inside the chassis of the car somewhere. Maybe inside the door frame or inside the engine block, somewhere that would be impossible to get to. That way the thing would rattle like crazy but be impossible to find. If they were going to fix it—and they'd have to—they were going to have to take the car completely apart. And when they would finally find the hanging bolt, they'd also find a little note that we'd attach to it that said: AHA! YOU FOUND ME!

I thought that was great because it was just a little bit of a private revolution by those guys. Here they were, every day, five days a week, screwing the same nut on the same bolt on the same spot on the same car a thousand times a day. It was their way of saying, "You treat us like machines. This is our way of showing you that we're humans." And I loved the thought of people going crazy trying to find the noise. "Where the *hell* is that rattle coming from?"

Well, that pissed GM off, to say the least. They threatened to kill their summer job program with Switzer. *Car and Driver* even did a big story on it, wanting to know if it was true. GM, or course, was backpedaling their ass off in Detroit. They said it wasn't true, but I know better. It was true. I saw it happen. I'm sorry if they didn't want it to come out. But, like I say, they forced my hand. They cheated me and they paid.

Most jobs GM gave OU football players were on the assembly line, but mine was delivering repainted parts around the plant. Say a door gets a chip in it. They'd paint a new one and I'd deliver it. Usually, though, there wouldn't be much to deliver, so I'd just sit on the bench in the back all day, playing dice and falling asleep. When they did have a part to send out, I'd get in my little golf cart and deliver it. Okay, okay, I'd take some detours. Like I'd always go see my buddy Greg Johnson over in body. They put him in body because he had the biggest body of anybody in the plant. He was an offensive tackle who weighed 320 pounds. He was in charge of lifting up Chevettes or something. Or I'd visit Al Laurita, one of our offensive guards. They put him back in the seal line because he's so short and squat, perfect for putting seal in a car.

Well, some of the guys didn't like how long it was

taking me to deliver these parts, so the foremen all of sudden put me on the line, even though it was against union rules. You can't just change a guy's job like that without going through a whole big process. I knew because, with all the time I'd spend on the bench in the back, I read the union rule book. So I protested. I told the guy, "I'm giving you thirty-minute notice. I'm going home sick."

When I came back the next day, there was a big inquiry. And the foremen told me he wanted me to sign a voluntary quit form.

"Forget that," I said. "I'm not voluntarily quitting. Now if you all want to lay me off, you can do that and I'll file a grievance with the union, saying you purposely laid me off."

"Sign it."

"Screw you. The way I look at it, I'm laid off."

So I walked out and a few days later I put the grievance together and I won $1,200 in back pay.

But they didn't pay. Instead, they called Switzer and said, "If Bosworth makes us pay him $1,200 in back pay, you can forget about getting other players jobs."

So Switzer asked me to forget about it and I said, "Okay, I'll forget about the money. Even though I need it. Even though it's mine. But they're going to get theirs in the end."

And that's when I told the truth about the hanging bolts in *Sports Illustrated*.

That didn't come out until two years later and by then I'd already established myself as someone who could get in trouble faster than you could say, "Switzer wants to see you."

I guess it all started that next year, just before the

Texas game. The writers were starting to talk to me about stuff because I'd been playing pretty well. I'd started my first game ever in OU uniform—at home against Stanford. I'll never forget that. The biggest crowd I'd ever played before in my life was ten thousand and here I was walking out at Owen Field and seventy thousand people screaming their hair off. I was scared to death.

And I remember on the first drive John Paye, the Stanford quarterback, completed three passes and—boom—they were in the end zone. I'm going, "Looks like I should've gone to A & M."

But then we started putting pressure on them, blitzing them from the inside, using our quickness, jumping in Paye's face. By the second quarter he was totally intimidated. He threw up a duck farm the rest of the day and we won, 19–7. I even got an interception that game. Murphy tipped it up and I got it. I thought, "Damn, interceptions are easy." How was I supposed to know I'd never get another one during my whole Oklahoma career?

The next week we kicked Pitt's ass and Bill Fralic's ass, 42–10. Then we killed Baylor, 24–15, in Norman, which was only memorable for what happened to Mig. Mig got knocked out so dead-ass cold that they weren't even sure they could wake him up. He'd made an interception for a touchdown earlier in the game, but after he got knocked out he couldn't remember a thing. As the game was winding down, he came up to me and said, "Did I make an interception today?"

And I said, "Oh, Mig! You don't remember? You were the damn star of the game! Not only did you make an interception, but you returned it for a touchdown! Then you returned another interception for a touchdown and, just before you got knocked out, you caught a fumble in midair and ran ninety yards for another touchdown! Man, they say you set some kind of record today!''

And Mig goes, "I did? Really?"

"Really!"

It was hilarious. I went around and had everybody go up to him and congratulate him. "Great job, Mig." "Fantastic. Never seen a game like it!" The next day in the papers, there's all these quotes from Mig about how it was the greatest day in his life and he just wanted to thank his teammates and stuff. We didn't tell him the truth until two days later. Boy, was he pissed.

Then we thumped Kansas State the next week, 24–6, and that was my introduction to how worthless some Big Eight programs can be. Playing Kansas State is about as exciting as visiting a great aunt in a nursing home. They were pathetic. They didn't even deserve to have a football team. It wasn't really the players' fault. It was the coach's fault, Jim Dickey. He had the worst schemes I've ever seen. They fired his ass the next year. He's probably running the IRS now.

We felt the worst for them because of their helmets. They were these ugly gray things that weren't even gray, really. They were sort of like the paint your father has out in the garage that he never uses. And their football stadium is an embarrassment to college football. I've seen better toxic waste dumps. No wonder Dorothy wanted to get the hell out of that state.

So that brings us to Texas and a couple of writers

came up to me and said, "You're from Irving. How come you didn't go to Texas?"

Dumb me. I've always thought if somebody asked you a question and you knew the answer to it, you should go ahead and give 'em the answer, not some company line, according-to-policy mumbo jumbo. But, I found out much later, that's not the way things work. Truth doesn't matter to most people. Politics matters. Stroking people's egos matters. But I didn't care then and I don't care now. If I know the answer, I give it. That's what going to school is all about, right? So I said, "I didn't go to Texas because I don't like Texas. I don't like Fred Akers. I don't like the city of Austin. And I don't like their color of orange. It reminds me of puke." Was that clear enough, you think?

I took some serious hell for that, and I admit I was wrong about Akers. I said I don't like him. I'd like to retract that. I *hate* him. His own players hate him. They'd tell me what a jerk he was. They'd say that sometimes, if the game wasn't going right, he'd get pissed and chuck the game plan and start calling stuff that didn't even make sense. Like on third and seventeen, he'd run a halfback dive. He'd do it just to show the players he was pissed. Sort of an adult temper tantrum. All that does is screw up the players. Gene Chilton, one of their stars, used to tell me, "I hate playing for that dumb shit Akers. He doesn't know a damn thing about football."

That was his ignorance. His arrogance was the way he and his staff recruited. Like how they called me up and asked if I could set up a trip to Austin.

"No thanks," I said. "Not interested."

Then later, I canceled a trip to SMU and they called right after that, hitting on me again.

"Since you canceled to SMU, would you like to come up just for the weekend?"

"No thank you."

But they didn't like taking "No thank you" for an answer. Akers's head recruiter starts ragging on me.

"How could you turn your back on your own state? You're a traitor. Listen, son. You need Texas. We don't need you."

I should've said, "Not anymore. Freddy needs *me* more than I need him." And nowadays, after what Freddy did to them, they *really* need somebody.

That's typical UT arrogance, typical of the whole university. I mean, I like Texas. I like rednecks and most of the people in that state. Real people. But I don't like UT alumni, who think just because they went to UT they're better than anybody else. Whenever someone comes up to me and says, "Would you give me an autograph, even though I *did* go to Texas?" I say, "That's all right. We're all allowed to make a few mistakes. Unfortunately, you have to live with yours the rest of your life."

So the next day I was amazed at how much of a splash my Akers quote made in the papers. I guess that's when The Boz was born, that day. That should show people The Boz is genuine. Brian was saying the same exact stuff in high school, except that nobody was around with pencils and pads, writing it down and turning it into The Boz quotes. The Boz was never *allowed* to come out before. But now he was out and I wasn't ashamed of it.

After that the writers started calling me "Bulletin Board" Bosworth. But Switzer never got mad. In fact, our coaches thought it was hilarious. According to UPI, we were the number two team in the nation and Texas was number one, but it didn't seem to bother the coaches. So much for the importance of keeping stuff off other teams' bulletin boards. That went out in the 1950s. Once you're in a game, what somebody else said about you lasts for about one hit. After that you're not going to be inspired by something you read in the morning paper. If you need *that* to get inspired, it's too late anyway.

The guys were getting off on it too. I became sort of their unofficial spokesman. I was a walking *Everything You Always Wanted to Say in the Papers but Were Too Afraid to Try* book. ''Hey, man,'' somebody would say. ''Why don't you tell 'em this?'' And it would always be some line that would get me thrown in jail. They wanted me to dog every head coach we'd play. But that's not how I felt about every head coach. Just Akers. And maybe Jimmy Johnson at Miami. The mole.

So now the pressure is on me to play well against Texas. I've got everything on the line now. I even get a death threat. Like the Texas game isn't already enough pressure. The students at both schools go crazy. Everybody's drunk all week long. They even call off school on Thursday and Friday. They play the Texas school song over the intercom while we're practicing. Even the three-hour drive from Norman to Dallas is amazing. Everybody goes all at once in this giant caravan. There's one fraternity that runs the whole way down there, each guy getting out and running two miles and then getting back in the van. Then he drinks about forty beers until it's his turn again.

By halftime of the game, we were behind, 10–0, on a flukey touchdown. I was really pissed as we all walked up the ramp together. I was screaming at the Texas players, "Merry Christmas. I hope you like your gift." Then somebody on their team went for my throat and they broke us up. But I think that energized everybody. That pulled us together.

We got right back into the second half when I hit their halfback at their own two. He fumbled and Keith Stansbury landed on it. We scored right away. At the end, we ended up holding them on one of the best goal-line stands I've ever been a part of. We were ahead, 15–10, and they've got a first and goal at the one. It was raining and we were all dog-tired, but I remember looking at everybody and they all still had a spark in their eye. Akers tried three running plays up the middle, and then, for some weird reason, he showed his brilliance by running a sweep. Nice one, Einstein: a sweep on a wet field that's slippery as snow. The guy just fell down without being touched. We took a safety and punted, but those pussies kicked a field goal at the end and, after some of the worst calls in modern officiating history, tied it, 15–15.

After that we went back on the YMCA League circuit again. We beat Iowa State in Ames, Iowa, one of the most godforsaken places on earth. Unfortunately, Danny Bradley, our quarterback, broke his index finger in that game and sat out the next game against Kansas. Troy Aikman took his place and guess what? We got beat. Undefeated going into the game and we got beat. And the worst part is that Kansas didn't get diddly the whole game. We gave them four first downs, total. What they did get was two interceptions returned for touchdowns and a fumble on our seven-yard line. I felt like drop-kicking Toto.

We took out our frustrations on Missouri the next week, 49–7, and then pummeled Colorado, which was running some derelict T-bone offense I'd never seen before or since. I think Alonzo Stagg invented it. We still had a chance at the Big Eight championship if we could win the next two—Nebraska and Oklahoma State. Only trouble is, Nebraska was ranked number one in the country that year and everybody was giving us no shot. No shot at all.

But what they don't know is that we had a hole card. We knew all of Nebraska's audibles. In fact, we knew all their audibles all three years I played Nebraska. It didn't help a whole lot, but at times it did. Like one time we heard what it was—Blue 29—and we yelled at our corner Jim Rockford, "Here it comes, Rock! Down and out!" And sure enough Rock stepped in front of it and picked it off. Nebraska must've thought they were playing a bunch of junior Kreskins or something.

That was a tough gut-busting game, one of those games where you don't even know what quarter it is. We were just so caught up in it, going so hard, that we lost all sense of time. It all came down to another goal-line stand, with us leading, 10–7, and Nebraska on our six. They started with a sweep, which we ran out of bounds. On second down they tried an option run. I stuck the hell out of the quarterback, if I do say so myself. Dante Jones stuffed 'em on a trap play on third down.

That brought up fourth down, game on the line, Big Eight title on the line, championship of the free world on the line. The Nebraska quarterback, Travis Turner, comes up the line and guess what he does?

Audibles!

"Black 19! Black 19!" he hollers.

Everybody on our team knew what Black 19 was—their patented pitchout to Jeff Smith. We stuffed Jeff's football where the cornhusks don't grow and won, 17–7. I had nineteen tackles and got Big Eight Defensive Player of the Week. I was disheartened to hear there was no cash award.

And when we beat third-ranked Oklahoma State the next week, the final regular season game of the year, it was Chivas time. We had the Big Eight championship and the Orange Bowl at stake and we just flat schooled 'em. We held them to minus four yards rushing. Of course, I was never worried because we were playing the Aggies, and the Aggies gag more in Norman than Reagan reaches for the Grecian Formula.

My dad came in the locker room afterward and we hugged and we both cried. That may have been the greatest feeling I ever had. It was the first time I'd won anything in football. It was a real emotional moment, the first time I realized I'd made him really proud. Finally it felt like number one *was* good enough. That felt even better than the national championship. That was probably the closest we've ever been as father and son.

But that was our season right there. Print it. We had our Big Eight title. Switzer was still gainfully employed. We went to Miami to play Washington for a chance at the national championship. Number one BYU was 12–0 after having beaten the Little Sisters of the Poor or something, so they could've been knocked off. All we needed to do was beat Washington bad and we could've won enough votes to win it. The voters didn't really want BYU, but they didn't have much choice. Only thing we had to do was impress some damn journalists. So what did we do instead? Party time. Chase biff. Drink every drink. Practice like turds. We were there to *celebrate*, not win. I was having so much fun I even got away with the world's most violent cake fight.

I still don't know where we got it, it was tradition among us that whenever somebody got sent a cake by a fan, it was to be destroyed in the most vile way possible. Well, Mig got a cake and I was rooming with him at the Fountainbleu Hotel in Miami and we had a slight altercation with it. By the time we were done, the beds were upside down, the mattresses were up against the wall, the sheets were torn up, cake was in the drapes and the carpet, water had soaked the wallpaper, and there was a hole in the wall. We were scared to death, but when we came back from practice the next day the place was spotless, as though nothing had happened. Very considerate. A miracle, in fact.

Football? Who needed to think about football? We figured we could beat Washington just on form. They weren't even the Pac 10 champions. They were the damn runners-up. Runners-up? We could beat runners-up in our bathrobes. So what did they do? They came out with running plays we hadn't even studied. They came out and kicked our butts. Really, we got ourselves outcoached. Not that I was any help. My legs felt like a dead cow's because I'd partied the whole week. That was the worst game of my career. If I had one game to do over, it'd be that one. Also, if I had that game to do over, I'd take the Sooner Schooner, fill it full of lighter fluid, and set a match to it. That damn Schooner came out on the field too soon to celebrate one of our field goals, pushing us back ten yards for the rekick, and we missed it. We ended up losing, 28–17. I may leave one of those ponies' heads in President Horton's bed some day.

Even after we lost, it didn't hit us. We went to some function they had for both teams and Mig and I went straight to the bar and just started slamming Scotch. I saw Gibbs and apologized for letting him down. He apologized to me for something else. We were both three sheets to the wind. I was so drunk that for some reason I found myself on a bus, all by myself, telling the driver I was ready to go home.

"You sure?" he said.

"Yep," I said, sounding like Goofy. "Ready to go."

"All right then," he said reluctantly. "You're sure?"

"Yep. All set to go."

He drove me back and when I got upstairs to my room I saw that it was only eight o'clock. And everybody I knew in Miami was still at a party I had no idea how to get to. That still remains the earliest I've been to bed since sixth grade.

Another player had the strangest story of all, though. He got so drunk that he went home with some girl he'd never met before. When he woke up the next morning, he said he was butt naked and didn't know where he was or who he was with. He looked around for his clothes, found them on the floor, and put them on. He looked around some more and saw that the girl was taking a shower. Then he saw some car keys on the counter and he took them. The keys said FORD on them, so he left the apartment, took the elevator to the bottom floor, and found the parking lot. He started looking around, trying the key in every Ford until he found one it fit. Then he just started driving until he saw something he recognized and made his way back to the hotel. He left the car in the hotel parking lot with the keys on the dashboard and came up to the room. That's it. He still has no idea who the girl was or where he was or if she ever got her car back. We must've laughed about that for an hour.

Still, I always felt a little sorry for that girl. She gets out of the shower and the guy that had been there two minutes before, the guy maybe she was going to start a new life with, was gone. And so was her Ford.

But I suppose the whole team felt sort of the same emptiness the next morning themselves.

That's when we realized we'd just thrown away a national championship.

CHAPTER
7

Say It's So, Joe

There I was, running out of my best "A" material. And there he was, Alonzo Highsmith, star fullback for the Miami Hurricanes, running out of *his* best "A" material. It was October 19, 1985, the game of the year. Owen Field was busting at the seams. We're number one in the country and undefeated. Miami is undefeated. And both the teams are at each other's throats. Only Alonzo and I are fresh out of disgusting things to yell at each other. So I yelled something like "When I'm done with you, you're going to have to fart to look out." And then I think he said it was too bad about my dog giving me AIDS.

And the weird thing was that they hadn't even flipped the coin yet.

That was the day we lost the game—and won the national championship. I know that sounds screwed-up, but it was a screwed-up year, a terrific, insane, wonderfully screwed-up year.

Not that it started so great. My knee was still hurting like crazy from the Washington game—even into spring ball. It hurt so damn much I didn't know what to do with it. The coaching staff wanted me to have arthroscopic surgery done on it. It's not like big-time, kick-ass surgery, just a little needle that goes

111

in and probes around and cleans it up. But it still scared the hell out of me. I'd never had an operation done on my body and I didn't want to start now.

So, instead, I kept going up to Oklahoma City and having it shot full of cortisone. Getting a shot of cortisone is the most painful thing in the world because that needle is about seventeen inches long—well, maybe not seventeen inches, maybe four inches long, but it feels like seventeen. I remember Coach Dan Pickett telling me, "Look, if you don't go in and get it scoped and find out what's wrong, then you're just going to keep going up there every week and getting cortisone shot in your knee." That changed my mind real quick. They gave me some drug before the operation that I'd love to bottle. That felt *gooooood*. And thank The Big Home Boy Upstairs that there was nothing wrong with it. I came home and I rehabbed for four weeks and I went out and went through spring ball.

So what happens? Some big doofus landed on my ankle during spring ball and sprained the hell out of my Achilles tendon, so then I had to rehab that. And I'm thinking, "Jesus, maybe I should just go back to the Orange Bowl and start over." That whole summer people are talking about what a great year I'm going to have. Reporters are coming down and I'm getting a lot of ink. I guess because I was the Big Eight Newcomer of the Year. They were saying I was the best Oklahoma linebacker since Rod Shoate. But here I was, worrying if I would even get the year in at all. I worried all through the summer because I couldn't twist my foot sideways. But then, *violà*, I started to get better. It finally worked its way out. I was one happy camper.

Now all we had to do was see who wanted to win a national championship. It was a strange collection of guys too. There were big old farm boys—like Stevie Bryan—and inner-city blacks—like our magician quarterback, Jamelle Holieway, who came from Watts in L.A. There were smart guys—like Tillman and Gatewood—and there were guys with boxes of rocks for brains—like our All-Galaxy nose guard, Tony Casillas, now with the Atlanta Falcons.

Okay, maybe I'm being unfair to Casillas. But there were only a few guys I didn't get along with on the team and Casillas was one of them. Casillas was just dumb. He screwed up and let his wife negotiate his pro contract. So he's stuck in Atlanta with a contract that pays him like a part-time Burger King cook. It's too bad because he's a damn good football player. Then again, Tony never was a candidate for brain surgeon or anything. You put a microphone in front of him and all of a sudden his brain shorts out. He rattles on and on and doesn't say a damn thing. People would say Casillas made it easy for me. That was bull because it was easier *after* he left than it was when he was there.

He was jealous of me, the fact that I was the leader of the class that sort of took over during his senior year. He was Mr. Established and I stepped in as a sophomore and took over. Kevin Murphy, our All-American linebacker, used to go at it with me a lot over Casillas. Murphy used to say if it wasn't for Tony I wouldn't be worth a damn. I said if he and Tony and his class were worth a damn, then Oklahoma wouldn't have gone 8–4 three straight years. It was *our* class that turned things around and he knew it. I told him, "You play by *our* rules. We don't play by your rules.'' That pissed *all* the seniors off, mostly because it was the truth.

We had a slight other problem on the team too: drugs. Some guys, especially some of the city guys, would freebase a lot of cocaine. One day I happened to see them doing it on the day of the game. I'm not one to preach to anybody, not with all the stuff I've done. And if those guys wanted to freebase hubcaps, they could, for all I cared. It was their choice. My thing is the individual. Whatever he wants to do is his decision. But freebasing on the day of the game really pissed me off. I teed off on them. I said, ''At least come to the game with a clear head. There's a lot riding on this season.'' I never saw it happen on game day again.

I'm not 100 percent simon-pure myself. My first year in college, with no football to go to, I got a little wild, but my body is my meal ticket, I wasn't going to tear it down. I drank too many of my dad's peanut butter shakes to screw the damn thing up now.

Anyway, that was the year the big suits in the president's office at Oklahoma sold out to national television and kept us penned in for about three weeks longer than anybody else. We were supposed to open the season with SMU, but in order to cash in big-time, the two schools agreed to move the game to the end of the season (we used to always end with Oklahoma State; so much for tradition) so that it would be televised on ESPN, meaning more money for everybody but the players, who were given exactly zero percent of the extra cash gained at their expense.

That meant that, instead of starting when everybody else did, we had to sit around three extra

weeks, since we had an off week scheduled after the
SMU opener. That meant we had four weeks of
training camp, twenty-eight days. We had a big sign
on the wall: 28 DAYS TILL MINNESOTA . . . 27 . . .
26 . . . We scrimmaged all the time against our third-
string quarterback, Eric Mitchell, who was damn
good. He had to be the best athlete in the country
not starting at *some* position. He just didn't have that
Jamelle magic. Of course, none of us knew what
that magic was yet. Jamelle was backing up Troy
Aikman, who was going to bring something strange
and new to Norman, Oklahoma: the forward pass.

By the time we opened our season at Minnesota,
we were the most bitchingest, raggingest, orneriest
group of people you'd never want to be around. So
what did we do? We went to Minnesota and looked
like gophers, barely winning, 10–7. I don't know if
we'd waited so long that we forgot how to play the
stupid game or what, but we stunk worse than some
of Mig's practice socks. Wouldn't it have been funny
for the big suits to have paid all that money to see
us play at the end of the year and we go out and lose
in the first game of the year?

Troy took a horrible beating that game because
he's white and he's tall and he's slow and can't run
a damn wishbone. He can throw like crazy, but he
can't run the wishbone. It'd be kind of like Vinny
Testaverde trying to run the wishbone. Starting Troy
might go down as one of the dumbest ideas in history, next to the guy who invented the NCAA. Then
again, I don't know what other choice Switzer had.
Jamelle was a true freshman and no way was he
ready to play.

Personally, I didn't play well in the game at all.

My head was in Timbuktu or someplace. I have no idea why. And that meant the whole next week I was miserable because anytime I had a bad game I'm just hell on myself and anybody that comes near. I take it out on my girlfriend or my parents or anybody that has the misfortune to cross my path. I'm a real ass for a week. Not only that, my ankle didn't seem to be coming back like I thought it would. I was depressed.

So that's when I decided to get my haircut in a most strange manner, according to most people. I was pissed off. I was outraged at the week before. I wanted something new. I wanted *something* to change. I needed some kind of motivation to get me going. So I guess you could say my haircut is a statement of rage. It has nothing to do with getting attention. I didn't do it for attention. I did it to change my way of thinking.

That haircut and a little dose of Kansas State and I was like new. Same ugly helmets, same ugly offensive scheme. But the thing that pissed me off more about them than anything is that all their players wear Converse basketball shoes. Don't ask me why. It's like they can't afford real football shoes. In our real football shoes, we kicked their ass.

Next week is the Texas game and my run of luck held out. I got the flu. I was sick as a dog. Plus, I took untold grief for my haircut. So my life is really going good. I can't even get out of bed, can't practice that week, and people are abusing me about my hair. But the chance to humiliate Fred Akers is the best medicine I could have. By game time I'm feeling slightly better and once I got out on the Cotton Bowl field I felt great. I don't know why, but I had maybe the greatest game of my life that day. Everything went right, from the very first play of the game, when Mr. Phi Beta Kappa, Akers, runs the very first play right at me. I'm shocked. No way he's that stupid.

Just to make Freddy pay, I stood the guy up and drove him back and, even though I heard whistles, I said to myself, "What whistles?" I drove him back, pile-drove him, and then screamed into his face, "This is gonna be one long day for you, son of a bitch." It's on that play that Casillas got clipped on the side of the knee and went out for two games. I really missed him. I didn't even notice he was gone until four series later.

Anyway, we went in at halftime of the Texas game and the score was 7–7. It was so hot that day I cut part of my jersey off to cool off, starting something of a minor tradition around OU. On hot days all the guys would be cutting the bottoms of their jerseys off. Pissed off the equipment staff, though. So what? Take it out of our $10 million.

Switzer never gave us any big halftime speech. In fact, Switzer hardly ever said anything at halftime. He just smokes his cigarette and listens in while the position coaches go over what we're doing wrong. Switzer isn't a coach. Switzer is a recruiter with a big office and a big name. But he's the best recruiter in the world.

The rest of the way we gave them nothing but our motto for the season: "Three and out." Three downs and we're off the field. Love it. We beat the mucus out of them. Toward the end of the game, I smashed their Mc-Quarterback, Todd Dodge, who stands just slightly taller than the cardboard clown kids have to be bigger than before they can get on a roller coaster. After I waylaid him, I turned him over and just went nuts on him. I'm yelling, "Don't you ever blankety-blank try to throw the ball again because I'm gonna kill you and all your blankety-blanks if you do!" And poor Dodge was just trying to find his mouthpiece. I think it was up the side of his helmet somewhere. I hit him so hard I thought he might sue me for whiplash. But then I got mine because Murphy came up and strangled me from behind. He was all pumped. He'd never beaten Texas before. None of the seniors had. And I'm choking to death—seriously. I'm hollering at him with one eighth of a windpipe, "Murphy! Let me go!"

We win, 14–7, and I'm so damn happy I could cry. After the goal-line stand I just went crazy and I ran about twenty yards and went sliding across the turf for about another twenty. It was weird because I'd dreamed about doing that the night before. Just one long, happy, soggy belly flop. It was such a big deal for me to beat Texas. That win was the sweetest victory I'd had since the Nebraska game my freshman year. It meant more to me, really, because of what was at stake. We gave them minus twenty-four yards, total offense. I had two sacks. I got the CBS Player of the Game. Switzer is delirious. He's kissing me on the cheek and telling the reporters, "That's the greatest performance I've ever seen a defensive team play and Boz is the greatest bleeping linebacker I've ever bleeping coached." I took that as a real compliment, coming from someone who's coached as many great players as Switzer. It was a big moment in my life. I'd had so many things go wrong. Now to get everything turned around, it felt so good.

Too good. That was the one week I let all the headlines and handshakes get to me. I had a head you couldn't fit through a garage door. I was starting to get a lot of serious media attention. And it was the first real national attention that I felt like I really deserved. So I went with it. That was the biggest mistake I ever made.

Because as big as the Texas game was to me personally, it wasn't a big a game nationally as the next one, Miami. But I walked around like I was Joe King Stud. I was like "I'm good. I'm cool. Brent said so." I did interview after interview that week. I took the game seriously, but not like what it deserved. I changed all of that right after that game because I realized what I'd done. But if I could live a week again, I'd relive that one.

Right away, the Miami game was like that last day of Saigon and we hadn't even kicked off yet. Guys that weren't out there flipping the coin are halfway across the field screaming. I guess it's not that surprising. These are two teams that, mentally, were identical. We both had made our reputation as teams that took no shit off anybody. They weren't backing down and we weren't either. Highsmith and I were face-to-face from the minute we got on the field. He was out on the field and I didn't think he should've been. So, of course, I went way out on the field to tell him to get off the field. Makes a lot of sense. I was flipping him off, telling him to get his big ass back on the sideline where it belonged. He was insisting I was also in violation of the rules as well. If Pete Rozelle had been there, he'd have fined us both.

That's weird, me yelling at Alonzo so much, because I respect Alonzo as a person and as a player. If you've ever talked to him, he's smart as hell. He's also one of the few guys who's never backed down from me. He's built like a damn building, so why should he back down? I found out later why I like Alonzo. In high school he played linebacker.

Alonzo did something to me that game I'd never had done before or since. He knocked me on my ass twice on one play. Twice! On one play! And then he gave me The Boz treatment.

"You low-life. I'll keep knocking your ass down, too, so you might as well just stop getting up, asshole."

Sounds like something off my greatest hits album. But the next quarter I hit him so hard he had to leave the game. He was hurting too. So I said, "Take your candy ass out of the game, you crybaby." Other than that, we were great friends.

Then Vinny came out, quiet as a mouse, and made everything pointless. He was death. He threw strikes. He could've beaten just about any NFL defense that day. He hit three beautiful TD bombs. He threw a pass to Michael Irvin that still brings tears to my eyes. It just couldn't have been thrown any better. The coverage was there. He just could not have thrown the pass any better.

But the funny thing was, Troy came out every bit as hot. If Troy had stayed in the game, we'd have won it. But if Troy hadn't gotten hurt, we wouldn't have won the national championship.

I know that sounds cold and all, but when you think about it, it's true. We won the national championship that year because we did what Oklahoma does best—we ran the bone. You can't beat anybody passing half the time and then trying to run the bone the other half with a white guy who takes October to get down the line. You need somebody with Jamelle's magic.

When Troy went out, Jamelle had no chance, of course. He wasn't ready to play right then, and we lost. But Switzer and Jim Donnan, our offensive coordinator, did an unbelievable job with him. They simplified the offense. And then, because we had a weak schedule after that, Jamelle got in a lot of practice and a lot of time in winning games, so it really built his confidence up. And we got our act together as a team too. We called a meeting after the Miami loss and said, "Look, let's just take care of our business—one week at a time—and we'll still get our chance." Translated: "Let's hire someone to kill Vinny."

Still, we'd lost in Norman and to me it felt like a two-iron in the head. It was the only time I ever lost at home and I started freaking. My mind was like sponge cake. I can hardly remember any of that next week.

I do remember that I'd never been more pissed at our fans than the next week. We played Iowa State at home and we go out for warm-ups and I look up in the stands, and they weren't even full. That really hacked me off. That was the first time I'd ever been disappointed in our fans. I know it wasn't just because we were playing Iowa State, which we beat, 59–14. I guess people were bruised because we lost against Miami. Damn people were spoiled.

Then we killed Kansas, 48–6 (as payback for screwing up the season before), and then Missouri,

51–6. Jamelle ran all over them, running the bone like he'd been doing it since kindergarten. It's amazing to me, even today, how he could do all that as a freshman. He'd cut back across the grain on a play that was going nowhere, something a freshman just can't do yet. I think what was working for him was his ignorance of the game. He didn't really know how hard it was *supposed* to be. Then we bombed Colorado, 31–0.

You can see how damn boring playing in the Big Eight can be. That year we beat everybody in the league, 270–39. In fact, they ought to just forget calling it the Big Eight. They ought to kick the junk schools out and make the division look a little better. They could call it the Big Three and the Little Five. The three would be us, Nebraska, and maybe a rotation between Colorado and Oklahoma State, whoever is any good that year.

I always thought the worst job in the world would be head coach at someplace like Iowa State or Missouri the Monday before they play Oklahoma. "Uh, okay, people? Listen up. Uh, we're playing Oklahoma this Saturday and we're going to get our asses kicked. Now, what I'd like you to do, as a favor to me, is not give up more than seventy points. I'd like to keep my job next year and my daughter just got her braces."

I feel bad for the players too. After about the first six minutes they just quit. They'll start out hard and we'll stuff their helmets down their throat and they just go, "Well, forget it then."

Our goals were entirely different for those games too. Gibbs would come into defensive meetings on the Monday before and say, "Okay, gentlemen. This

week our goal is to get negative yardage.'' That's
what it came down to. Trying to beat up the guy in
the stats booth. But Gibbs was maybe the only man
on earth who could get us to care enough to do it.
If Gibbs asked us to, we'd have swum through a pool
full of sharks in hamburger swimsuits. He was the
guy I turned to when I needed to get cranked up.
Our relationship started as business, but we ended
up as friends. And if Gibbs doesn't get the OU job
when Switzer leaves, then nothing makes sense in
the world.

Anyway, the fact that most of our Big Eight games
were like varsity versus junior varsity is what made
the Nebraska games so great. You're just so glad to
be picking on somebody your own size. Then again,
we were playing so good at this point we felt like it
was the Big One and the Little Seven.

The setup to the game was great. Nebraska was
pissed off at us because we took their title the year
before. The crowd was huge and incredibly loud. I
remember my first game in the Seattle Kingdome as
an NFL rookie and somebody said to me, ''Can you
believe how loud it is in here?'' I wanted to say,
''Man, this is a library compared to OU-Nebraska.''

Keith Jackson (six chapters later, I still don't know
why he came to Oklahoma) set the tempo for the
day by taking one of the first plays of the day for an
end-around touchdown. After that we just husked
their ears. We played great defense all day. We even
had a 27-0 shutout going with twenty-five seconds
left until some fat moronic Nebraska lineman, Chris
Spachman, caught a fumble in midair and took it all
the way in. There wasn't a damn thing we could do

about it on defense. We just stood there and watched our shutout vaporize. My chin was scraping on the AstroTurf. I'm running around, screaming at the offense, ''What the hell do you want to be carrying the ball around for with twenty-five seconds left, anyway?'' That ruined my whole game. That would've made four straight shutouts. Damn.

Now we're 8–1 and Miami has lost to Florida. So we're ranked third behind Penn State, who's undefeated, and Florida, who beat Miami. We've got two games left—Oklahoma State and SMU—and if we can win those, we've got a shot at the title because we know we're going to the Orange Bowl and Florida can't go to a bowl. All we needed was for Penn State to stay undefeated and agree to come to the Orange Bowl. *Puh-leeze.*

So we go to Stillwater for the OSU game and, just our luck, it's the worst weather there in years. People call it the Ice Bowl to this day. It was sleeting the whole time. It's cold as a damn icebox. It's the worst game I've ever played in. It's twenty below and God knows what the wind chill is. I put on as many shirts and jerseys as I could and it still didn't help. And everytime I came off the field, I couldn't even get a place next to the heater. It was like you had to take a number. I'd be surprised if Horton wasn't over there, warming his big butt. My fingers were frozen. We killed 'em, 13–0. Our streak of not giving up a touchdown went to twenty quarters. Not only that, but we won the Big Eight championship right then and there. It wasn't the Big Eight championship we were after, but it was still good news. In fact, I was so warmed by it, my Horton almost thawed.

So then we dusted off the best team money can buy, SMU, 35–13. Afterward, we got the news after that game that we were going to play Penn State in the Orange Bowl for the national championship.

I was so happy I almost said a prayer to St. Joe.

CHAPTER
8

The World
According to Me

Let me introduce you to two people: Brian and The Boz.

The Boz is the quotable, outrageous, occasionally obnoxious never-give-a-damn side of me. The Boz is the guy who's not afraid to be an individual in a world of automatons. Almost everybody has an opinion on The Boz.

Brian is the quiet, unobtrusive, very professional side of me. Brian likes nothing better than staying home, renting a movie, and putting his feet up. Almost nobody knows Brian.

I don't know when exactly it happened, but somewhere in there, The Boz became this giant symbol for people and Brian became forgotten.

To old farts or people who just think old, The Boz became the symbol of the anti-Christ, the symbol of everything that's wrong with everything, period. Every time I get a new design on the side of my head, ten thousand guys in John Deere hats go, "What'd I tell you, Merle? That there is another sure sign that boy is possessed by a demon."

To people under thirty, or people who still had an open mind, The Boz became a symbol for a new kind of hero: somebody who wasn't afraid to give the finger to The Way Things Are Supposed to Be and, at the same time, could still accomplish great things. Someone who could make it work his own way. I was a three-time All-American. I was a three-time Academic All-American too, a 3.3 student who graduated in four years with a degree in management information systems. Yet at the same time I stayed a hero to myself. I was still true to myself. I didn't play politics. I didn't suck up to anybody—anytime, anywhere. If something was wrong or unfair or stupid or ugly, I said so. If I enjoyed something, I got into it, no matter what somebody else thought.

But it wasn't until one day, the summer after we'd won the national championship, that I even realized there were two sides to me. My dad was reading the paper. I guess I'd said something outrageous in it and that's when he said, "Brian, you created this guy and now you have to live with him."

By *him*, of course, he meant The Boz, and he was right about having to live with it. But he was wrong about me creating him. I didn't create him. I've been like this since I was pedaling my trike down the Beltway.

Once The Boz started getting his opinions on life published in the papers—some of his philosophies on society and people—I started getting some wild reactions. I could be in some store and half the people would want my autograph and want to touch me and say, "Boz, we think you're the greatest thing since reservoir-tipped condoms." And the other half would want to have me arrested right there and then.

One time this old lady came up to me and said, "Do you know what you're doing to the kids of today, you Godless pig?"

"Yeah," I said, "I'm unlocking the door so they can get the hell out of *your* house."

I guess the way I go through life is an *attitude*. I think I've shown kids that they can think for *themselves* and still be good at what they do. That they can still *be* themselves. They don't have to dress a certain way, talk a certain way, hold their napkin a certain way to be a success in the 1990s. The old rules don't apply anymore. What counts is *results*. That's what I've learned from Switzer. That's why I like Al Davis's motto for the Raiders: "Just win, baby. I don't care what you did the night before. Just get it done today." That's sort of my motto: "You can be yourself. But you better be good."

I don't say why so many people are interested in how I live my life, but they are. I can go into a restaurant, and not only will the busboy know who I am, but the cocktail waitress, the maitre d', and the manager too. You'd be amazed how many people come up to me and say, "I don't know a thing about football, but I think you're terrific." Or ". . . but I think you're a total jerk."

I guess it's like a roadside collision. Some people can't help but watch me, even though they don't want to. People are always saying to me, "I've been following your act for years and I want you to know I think you're full of shit."

"If you think I'm full of shit," I always reply, "how come you've been following my act for years?"

And, of course, the reason so many adults know who I am and follow every move I make is because secretly they envy me. They envy my kind of life-style. Adults dislike The Boz because they see in him what they want to be, but can't. There they are, stuck behind a desk in the same gray suit and blue tie everybody else in the office is wearing, taking orders from somebody dumber than them, and they hate it and they'd like to go paint or start their own business or captain a sailboat or whatever, but they're too scared. They'd like to tell all the people in the corporation what they think of all their politics and hypocrisy and backstabbing, but they're scared they might lose their position in life. They don't have the balls. But kids do. Kids don't care. Kids haven't been robotized yet. Kids realize they have the world in their hands. It's kids who I care about because kids I can still reach.

People are always on my case about kids. I had one lady tell me, ''You're a terrible role model for kids. You're leading them the wrong way.''

That's bull. I think I'm a great role model for kids and if she'd ever thought about it, she'd agree. I've never been arrested. I don't do drugs. Never snort coke. Don't do heroin. One time, at this club in Oklahoma City, a guy came up to me while I was standing there, a real sleazoid.

''Hey, man, you want something?''

I knew what he was talking about. ''No thanks. Don't do that shit.''

''No,'' he said. ''It's cool. I'm low-profile.''

''Look,'' I said. ''I ain't gonna tell your ass again. Now leave me alone.''

He walked off, but later, in the bathroom, he came up to me again.

''Hey, man,'' he said. ''Everybody wants something. You gotta want *something*.''

The guy just chapped my ass, hassling me like

that, so I turned around and let my right fist party with his face. Knocked him down and out. Didn't feel bad, either.

That story ended up making the papers and kids saw that. If they think I'm cool, then they think it's cool to treat dealers like pond scum. And I do.

For another thing, I'm no tackling dummy. I got A's in both Calculus and Statistics. You try doing that and practicing football and watching films eight hours a day. My last semester at OU, my class schedule read like this: Management Information Systems, Finance, Insurance, Personnel Management, and Criminal Law. (Just in case I take something too far one night.) Sometimes that year I'd get out of practice, spring to the training table, eat the swill they gave us for dinner, and spring to a night class that I barely made. Other than that, I'm a lousy role model.

Somebody once said I was the last guy in the world most fathers would like to see on the other side of the door peephole waiting to take their daughter out on a date. I agree. To me, that's the ultimate compliment. I don't want fathers to like me. I want the daughters to. I don't give a rat's turd about what adults think about me because I don't want their approval. If anything, I want their *disapproval*. I want them to hate me, think I'm the root of all evil. The more adults think I'm the end of the universe, the better.

It's like one time a reporter asked me, "Do you think people think of you as a juvenile, immature, hated asshole?"

And I said, "I certainly hope so. I thrive on it."

To me, that's my *Good Housekeeping* Seal of Approval. It's like "Okay, let's see . . . All the tight-ass polyester adults in the Plymouths think this guy is a prick. He must be okay. Let him through."

Most adults who hate me are two-faced. They respect my personality in other people, but not in me. Anybody else they know that is a hard-driving, say-what-he-wants, win-at-all-costs achiever, they call "a great guy, tough as nails, really going places." But me they call "obnoxious, cutthroat, evil." That's because they consider sports a game, not a job. I should have them call my accountant.

My public image is so sharply divided between young people and old people that you could drive a Mack truck between the two. I mean, sure there are some old people who understand me and some young people who don't, but not many. The kids see the real me. How I dress. How I live. They think I'm cool-looking. They like the hair and the earrings and the clothes. I'm a success, drive a nice car, do what I want to make a living. Not afraid to speak my piece.

But the adults see this Neanderthal man. They expect me to walk around and drool and grunt and go by somebody's table in a restaurant, grab a piece of chicken, bite it, and toss it aside. They expect me to walk up, throw their daughter over my shoulder, punch out their wife, and Hulk-step it up to some cave. They don't know me, don't know anything about me. I'm not a barbarian. I'll bet you $100 I know my way around a wine list better than 99 percent of the people I talk to. I've visited more foreign countries than most people, met more interesting people, seen more, done more than 99 percent of the people who say I'm a vulgar animal. I subscribe to *Bon Appetit*, for Chrissakes.

Somewhere, some people got this barbarian image of me. They think of me as somebody who might come up and take a bite out of their nose. I've learned not to let it bother me, but it used to. Until the national championship, I'd almost had nothing but good press, people saying good things about me. But after that I started getting hate mail. And that bugged me. I didn't deal with it very well at first. One time somebody asked me one of those finish-this-sentence questions.

They said, "All right, this is you talking . . . 'I'd give almost anything to meet . . .' "

And I said, "Myself."

And it was true. *I* knew who I was, but I had no idea at that point how other people saw me. At that point, I still wanted everybody to like The Boz *and* Brian.

I remember telling my girlfriend one night, "Everybody knows The Boz, but nobody knows Brian. I guess I don't mind if they hate The Boz. But I don't want them to hate Brian." I didn't know then that what I wanted was totally imBozzible. Nobody's going to know Brian. For that matter, I don't *want* very many people to know Brian. I don't have time to convince people I don't fry up hamsters for dinner. The people I want to know Brian know Brian. Screw the rest. Those people are all I care about. And they seem to like me. I mean, they always send me Christmas cards.

Still, it bothered me for a while, being unliked, and I think one place I screwed up was with the press.

When I first started getting interviewed by writers, I figured this was a way I could get some attention for me and for Oklahoma and the guys on the team. I really wanted to put Oklahoma on the map. Well, I did that. No problem. And then pretty soon here I was, twenty-one years old, and people are coming out of the woodwork, coming from across the country just to interview me. They were coming to see what wild outrageous thing I'd do or say next.

Every time they asked me a question, they expected me to say something sensational, and I guess *I* expected me to say something sensational too. It got to where I felt I needed to feed my image, the image of The Boz, instead of what I had set out to do, sell OU. They weren't much help. They came to hear outrageousness, not the OU fight song. They came to hear me say something like "Texas reminds me of puke." I didn't make that up. That's how I feel. That's not a fabrication just to make a headline. And, yeah, that's part of me. But it's not the whole man. That's The Boz and The Boz is part of me, but Brian is part of me too. But the media really wasn't interested in Brian. They were interested in The Boz. I could understand it. After all, I was the one that didn't let them get to Brian.

But I never dreamed how many people take newspaper articles as Gospel. Especially the *Sports Illustrated* article. We did that tongue-in-cheek. I really didn't think people would take *everything* I said in there to heart. Like, now, people think if I get too close to them, I'll spit a loogie in their face and cuss. Hey, I'm a Christian. Would I do that? Don't answer.

But when someone sees a quote, they see it in

black and white. They don't see any color behind it. They take it literally. Everybody takes everything I say literally. That's because their assholes are *thiiiiiiis* tight. I remember this guy came up to me once in Oklahoma City and said, "I think you're a jerk."

"Why do you think I'm a jerk," I said.

"Because of what I've read in the paper."

"Do you believe everything you read in the paper?"

"No, of course not, but . . ."

"Do you think everything in the paper is pure fact?"

"No, but that has . . ."

"Do you know me? Have you ever talked to me before? Have you ever met me before? Do you know anybody who knows me?"

"No, but still . . ."

"End of conversation."

What would really bug me is when a reporter would come to hear me say outrageous things, and then, when I'd say them, he'd rip me. Like he'd ask me some blatantly leading question like "So, what do you think of Akers?"

Okay, I'll bite. I like to have fun. And I'd do the whole Akers thing. Then he'd rip me in the papers for mouthing off. Nice. In law, that's called entrapment. Either go along with the game or don't. That kind of shit burned me up because most writers told me they loved coming to Oklahoma because I'd fill up their notebooks for them. I'd give them something to write about. And I'd be candid, truthful, anything but boring. They knew when I talked to them, they weren't going to get some BS like

"They're a fine team. It's really a shame one of us had to lose."

Then, my last year at OU, Coach Gibbs came up to me and told me, "Brian, you're making it too easy for them [the press]. You're doing their job for them." And he was right. I suddenly realized I didn't have to make every writer's trip to Norman worthwhile. They could go look up some of the old stuff if they wanted some lines. I had a damn warehouse full. If I had something to say, I'd say it. I wouldn't hold back. But I finally stopped forcing things. I realized that all this time I thought I was using the media when it turned out the media was using me. Brian finally gave The Boz a few days off.

Some guys understood that. The writers understood that. The reporters didn't. You've got to realize there's a difference. Reporters are short fat "wanna-be's." They wanna-be players or they wanna-be coaches and they're pissed off they can't, so all they do is rip. If you ever need to find a reporter, you can find him hanging around any free lunch or hospitality room. Most columnists are just wanna-be's with their picture in the paper. Columnists are people who have an opinion on everything and don't know jack about what they're talking about. "Let's see. Today I think I'll be pissed off about Dan Rather. Don't know why, really. Never met the man. But it's two hours until deadline and I gotta think of something or they'll kick me back to the flower show beat." Most reporters are guys who would interview a widow before anybody had told her that her husband is dead.

Writers, on the other hand, are cool. Writers are professionals. For one thing, they can write—unlike reporters, who think they can write but instead just turn out volumes of phlegm. For another thing, writers don't look like Oscar Madison from "The Odd Couple." Some of them actually dress decently. For a third thing, they treat you like a professional. Guys like Steve Wieberg of *USA Today*, Skip Bayless of the Dallas *Times Herald*, TV guys like Dale Hansen in Dallas and Jerry Orr in Oklahoma City. Those guys I could respect. They weren't always complimentary, but they were always straight-up with me. Watch it, guys, you're giving the profession a good name.

Now I know exactly what my public image is and I don't care one way or another about it. I try to come off as myself in public, pure and simple. Sometimes that means I come off as The Boz and sometimes as Brian, depending on how I'm feeling, just like anybody else. I don't force anything anymore. I don't care if people hate me anymore. I even have ten rules of life I go by now, so that all the outside bullshit doesn't affect me and so that I'm true to myself.

The 10 Boz Commandments

1. Be yourself or be dead.

That's everything.

2. Cause change.

If you see a rule that doesn't make sense, a rule that's there just so somebody can wear an armband or print out a list of more rules, then break it. Protest it. Get rid of it. Kids need to learn to speak up for themselves. From letters kids send me I think my going on and on about how adults won't listen, how they don't have all the answers, has affected a lot of kids. They say they can express themselves much better now. They're not afraid to speak out about what they feel. They're not so all-willing to kneel down in front of authority. And why should they? Authority has done a pretty good job of screwing up the world so far.

3. Show some emotion.

Nobody wants to show emotion because everybody's afraid of looking the fool. When I get a sack or a really good hit, I just jump straight up in the air with my arms raised up. It's not premeditated. It's not like I'm thinking, "Got to do something for CBS now." It's pure 100 percent joy. I couldn't stop myself if I wanted to. So I get heat for this. One day, while we were playing Colorado in Boulder, I jumped up after a sack and their 30-IQ fans (all together) heaved all these oranges at me. (Those fans in Boulder are real Phi Beta Kappas. Later they threw a bottle at me and knocked out one of their own cheerleaders.)

When I have a son, I want him to give me a hug and a kiss on the cheek, no matter how old he is. If I'm sixty and he's thirty, I still want that hug. What's wrong with showing emotion, showing love, or anger or rage or happiness? They're natural emotions. They're what separates humans from lamps.

4. People that hate you hate themselves.

I think what really gets them about me is the $11 million. That really pisses them off. It's like Ray Nitschke, the old linebacker for the Green Bay Packers. He ripped into me publicly one day about my contract. He said he would never ask for that kind of money. Said he'd be too embarrassed. Now, I can see a fan saying something like that, but not a player. I could never begrudge another player making money. It's the market. If one guy gets more, it's only good for me. And here's Nitschke reaming me out about getting too much money. Can I help it if he was too dumb to ask for a decent wage playing for Green Bay? Obviously, he was pissed at himself for making peanuts all those years and now here I am, only twenty years later, making really good money.

He should be yelling at himself. Ray Nitschke is a fifty-year-old man with a three-year-old brain. And no hair.

5. Only one face to a person.

Two-faced people suck. That's one reason I like football. There's no hypocrisy in football. There's no looking at both sides of the ball. If there's a guy over there in an orange shirt and you're wearing green, then you go kick the ass of the guy in the orange shirt. Simple as that.

6. Never, ever, be bored.

I'd go over to John Elway's house and look at his home movies before I'd sit around being bored. And that's why so many people light into me all the time. Because *they're* bored and I'm not. They've got those desk jobs and the company suits and it pisses them off because it shows how boring their lives are. But, at the same time, I see people all the time who are fired-up. Fired-up about the game or fired-up about their job or being a success or fired-up about driving their car or whatever. They're involved in something. They're not like some of the moody selfish people who come up and bother me. People who are really into life don't have time to come up to me and tell me what they think of my latest sunglasses. They've got lives to live.

7. Only people you care about have opinions you care about.

This one took me a long time to learn. Take hate mail, for instance. At first it bothered me. I mean, until then, everybody loved me and that was great. Then it changed and I started getting hate mail from grandmothers. It used to be that if I pissed somebody off I dreaded it because that meant having to go through life knowing somebody hated me. It's not easy being the bad guy. But pretty soon I realized that some people only love you if you do it according to their rules. And if you do it according to their rules, somebody *else* hates you. Well, screw that. That's not natural for me. I'm not asking anybody else to change. So I gave up caring what people think of me.

Now I've gone 180 degrees from where I used to be. Now when I get mail, the first letters I pull out are ones from Colorado and Miami, the two places in the country where people hate me the most. You'd be amazed what people can write with Crayons. I pull that out and go sit on the john and read it because I know it's going to be the funniest stuff. Some of 'em have even contributed pictures, probably because the author was illiterate. Usually the picture features me, my mouth, and a giant penis. But I always have the last laugh. Because I know that when I come to his town, this same idiot that drew the picture is going to pay twenty-five bucks to come see if I fall on my face.

8. No preaching.

I know I'm not right 100 percent of the time and I know my particular lifestyle isn't for everyone. That's why I don't preach. That's why I don't idolize anybody and that's why I don't ask any-

body to idolize me. I've never asked anybody to
follow my way of life.

I don't buy it when people tell me a sports star
has a responsibility to be better than everybody
else. I don't want kids emulating me. I don't want
them emulating anybody. I simply want them to
be themselves.

9. Tell the truth.

I once read that people tell two hundred lies a
day in one little form or another. Like, say, Fred
comes up to Jack and says, "How do you like
my tie, Jack?"

"It's fine, Fred." But actually, Fred really
hates that tie. Has always hated ties like that.

Our society would rather lie than be honest.
And that's why they get on my case for speaking
up. My honesty bugs them, I guess. They think
I should just yammer on and on and not say a
thing, like just about everybody else in sports.
To me, that's the hope for the younger generation. They've got to have the courage to stand up
and say what they think, whether it's about nuclear weapons or South Africa or where they can
park their skateboard.

10. Kids matter.

I've given up on everybody but kids. Most
adults are so set in their ways that they're afraid
they'd be thrown out of their Kiwanis Club if
they start to think my ideas make sense. But
kids can still make it. If you can make them
think twice whether it's worth fifteen years of
hard work to blow something up their nose for

fifteen minutes of pleasure, you've accomplished something.

I can tell pretty quickly how a kid is doing with his parents as soon as they walk up to me. The parents who hate me are usually the parents whose kids are scared of them. They want to run their kids' lives, make them think *their* way. They're not friends, they're dictators, and as soon as the kid turns sixteen, he's going to start rebelling. It's always kind of sad.

I don't have a lot of compassion for people, but for kids I'm a sucker. One of my best buddies in the world is Brian Rothlein, a ten-year-old kid in Tulsa. I met him through Coach Marv Johnson at OU my freshman year. Marv said, "Hey, I've got a favor to ask you. There's this six-year-old kid who's fixing to go up to Boston to have open heart surgery and I don't think he's going to make it. He's requested that he'd like to spend some time with you."

"Sure," I said.

I wasn't playing in that spring game, so I hung out with him. I don't know why, but we hit it off. I let him ride in the Sooner Schooner, brought him into the locker room, and gave him one of the towels my Mom sewed for me that said BOZ, 44, OU. That was the only towel I've ever given out.

Brian had this defective heart. He'd had open-heart surgery when he was two and they never thought he'd make it to six. But I guess Brian doesn't give a rat's ass what other people think, same as me. He never let it enter his mind. So now he was going in for a heart transplant and his parents told me there was an 80 percent chance he wouldn't make it.

They said Brian took that towel with him into the operating room that day. His dad called me from Boston and said that the nurses had tried to take it away from him when he went into surgery, but Brian wouldn't let them. He just clutched that towel all the way through. His parents said they thought I inspired him to survive the surgery. I don't believe that. I think Brian is just a tough little cuss.

I know he is because after the surgery they said he'd only live six months. Well, he's ten now. I got a letter from him the other day and he's about to start playing T-ball. Can you believe that?

For somebody with a bunch of messed-up aortas and ventricles, that kid sure does have a lot of heart.

CHAPTER

9

Fame, Fortune, and Females

The best dang five-year-old halfback in the history of the Irving, Texas, YMCA Mustangs. Notice I hadn't hit enough people yet to scrape off those freckles.

Even at nine, I had a serious mean streak. And the worst thing is, this kid was on *my* team.

MacArthur High School graduation, 1983. I'm smiling because there's no diploma in there.

Would you let *your* daughter go to the prom with this man?

(UNIVERSITY OF OKLAHOMA)

Let's see. I'm bored. My uniform is still clean. And we're so far ahead I'm out of the game in the second quarter. Must be a Kansas State game.

Spring picture, freshman year. When people ask me why I changed my hair, I show them this picture.

(UNIVERSITY OF OKLAHOMA)

(UNIVERSITY OF OKLAHOMA)

Junior season, putting the hurt on Gaston Green of the UCLA girls' football team. The hardest hit I took that whole day was the one my pal, Paul Migliazzo, was about to lay on me from behind.

(UNIVERSITY OF OKLAHOMA)

Losing to Miami my sopho-
more year. They beat the shirt
out of us. I'm fixing to signal
another touchdown for Vinny
Testaverde.

(UNIVERSITY OF OKLAHOMA)

Lifestyles of the rich
and famous. Come to
Oklahoma, be an All-
American, and you, too,
can own a Corvette *and*
a Jeep. What sopho-
more doesn't need two
cars?

Here, I'm reminding Oklahoma State quarterback Mike Gumby, er, Gundy that it's third down and he still hasn't done anything right. Just trying to be helpful.

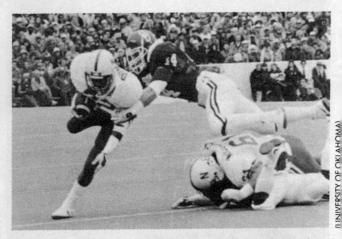

I hated Doug DuBose, a Nebraska running back, because he'd never let me swear at him. Every time I'd tackle him, he'd jump up and say, "Great play, buddy!" What a dirty trick.

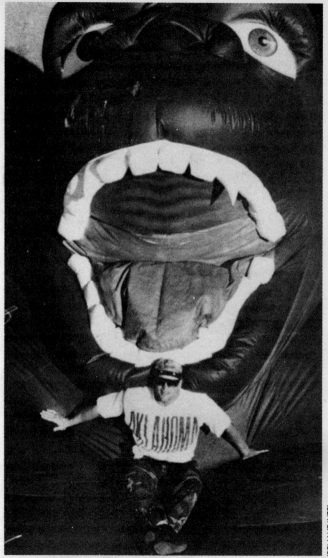

The only mouth in the world bigger than mine.

This is after we beat Texas, 14–7, my sophomore year. We held the Shorthorns to seven yards total offense. No wonder they call Fred Akers an offensive genius.

My first day at the Seattle Zoo. Here, I'm answering a question about nuclear disarmament.

Here I am at my $100-per-half-day college job watching an oil rig go up and down. Nice work. And no heavy lifting.

Coming soon to a theater near you.

Cardinal Rule: always wear sunglasses at press conferences. Too many ugly reporters in the world.

(UNIVERSITY OF OKLAHOMA)

Robocop to the rescue.

(UNIVERSITY OF OKLAHOMA)

Notice the protests on my wrists. Czar Rozelle put the slam on that too. See ya in court, Pete.

(CORKY TREWIN)

(CORKY TREWIN)

Me, wearing my wrong number. I only wish it was Pete Rozelle in that helmet instead of Marcus Allen.

(CORKY TREWIN)

A collector's item. Me, wearing my real number.

(CORKY TREWIN)

Coming off the field after we beat the Raiders in L.A. I'm smiling up at the only Raider fan that still has all his teeth.

(CORKY TREWIN)

Personally, I think this style could catch on.

My girlfriend, Katherine, makes it all worthwhile.

Here's me and my dog, Raider, in a stare down. He always blinked first.

THE LAND OF BOZ

MONSTER O.J.
44

BOZKIN
44

14

(PHOTO BY DOUG LANDRETH)   © 1987 COSTACOS BROTHERS ENTERPRISES

One reason I wanted to write this book is to clear up my image, let a little bit more of myself out. If you read the book and find out who I am and what I'm like and you still hate me, fine. Get in the back of that very long line over there. But maybe if you know me better you'll understand me better. Where's Phil Donahue when you need him?

The only thing I like as much as football is making love. Okay, I like it *better* than, say, a regular season game, but not the playoffs. I like to make love in romantic, exciting places. One place I have *not* made love is in a perfect stranger's house. Just walk in the front door of somebody's house you've never met, find a room, and make love. The danger is half the fun. Haven't been able to convince my girlfriend on that one yet.

I'm picky about women. I have this rating system. A woman's looks divided by her personality has to equal 1. What I mean is, she has to be as smart as she is good-looking, and she has to be kick-ass out-law good-looking. Because what I've found happens is that looks get old. Say I marry a fox, but her looks get boring. And she isn't smart, isn't sassy, doesn't challenge me mentally. Then the whole thing starts to drag on and pretty soon we're breaking up over who forgets to put the toothpaste top back on.

Italian women I love. They're beautiful and they're sassy because they were raised by Italian fathers. You've got to have someone you can spar with. The best of all, though, is an Italian blond woman with a tan and a beautiful body and, uh, one of those full figures Jane Russell is always talking about. When I run my hands over a woman's body, I like to have some varying degrees of altitude, you know?

Not that I'm doing my thesis on women's anatomies. I have one girlfriend, Katherine, right now and that's it. I don't want anyone else. When I'm at a club with my buddies, the most I like to do is look at women. Once they come up and start talking to me, it's usually ruined. That's because most of the time they're forward as hell.

One night me and my buddy were at this bar in Seattle. We were just standing against a wall, having a brew and talking. And this girl comes up to me out of the blue and says, "Boz, you just gotta lighten up." And she puts her hand right on my, uh, most personal limb, if you get what I mean. Just comes up and puts her hand right on my head coach. Like I'm not supposed to notice or I'm supposed to get off on it. "Oh, *dahhhling*. I love it when you treat me like a piece of flank steak. Your place or mine?"

It made me sick, partly because she was ugly. No, she wasn't even ugly. She was past ugly on to *ooooogley*. So I moved her hand and she just put it back. I finally had to walk away. I'm surprised she didn't keep it on there while I was walking too. I didn't need to loosen up, she needed to *tighten* up.

What if I had walked up and done that to her?

Twice! First of all, you'd have read about it in the morning paper. Second of all, I'd be in jail. Third of all, I'd go down as the biggest pervert since Lance Rentzel. But what happens when I ask this lady, politely, would she kindly remove her lovely hand off my joint if it's not too much to ask? She cops an attitude on me. She acts like maybe I've just slam-dunked her kitten. "I can't believe you!" she's screaming. "You're rude! You're a pig!"

"Right, sweetheart. And you're Miss Manners."

Guys always say to me, "Man, I bet you could get laid every night if you wanted to." Okay, I could, but so what? Who wants to nowadays anyway? I like to look at the car, but I won't go for a test drive. I don't take home *anybody* except my girlfriend.

To me, girls are just a pain in the ass. They call at all hours of the night. They knock on the door at four in the morning. They leave their phone numbers on my car. They leave notes with dirty messages on them. Do they think this gets me hot or something? Some perfect stranger leaving scumbag notes on my car? Like this is her way of us starting to go out, have a relationship. Like I'm going to introduce her to my parents someday. "Mom, Dad. This is Silver. We met after she left a note on my car saying she'd like to see me naked in a bathtub full of Malt-o-Meal." I mean, Christ.

And then if I don't call them or go out with them, they tell people I did anyway. I can't win. And boy does that piss my girlfriend off because she always ends up hearing about it through the rumor grapevine.

And if they're not being totally forward like that, then they're doing something else unattractive, like not being themselves. They're always trying to impress me. Telling me they're fixing on being a model or they *are* a model or they're an actress. Right. I'm in a Pittsburgh bar with eight girls who are currently working as actresses. *Right*.

People should just be who they are. I don't care what you're planning on doing. Go out and do it. Talk is cheap. If you have confidence about yourself, why do you come up to a complete stranger—me— and start telling me all about it?

It'd be impossible for me to date anyway. I could never trust the woman. I wouldn't know what she's hanging around me for. Back when I didn't have much money—well, not *as much* money—sometimes I felt women wanted to go to bed with me for my body. But now I think they try to go to bed with me more for the contour of my wallet than the contour of my muscles.

You just see it happen too much in the NFL. Guys go out with a girl one time and the next thing you know some guy in a three-piece suit is handing their ass a paternity suit. Or a guy makes it with a girl and all of a sudden she's charging him with sexual molestation because she knows he'll settle out of court for about $100,000. It's either that or get his name dragged through the papers and she knows it. I've seen it happen to too many guys.

In fact, if I ever get married, I might even consider signing a prenuptial agreement. You never know what happens down the line. Why should one person go into a marriage and come out better than she went in? Why don't you go in and come out the same way? I suppose I just made the *Ms.* magazine death watch.

Maybe if I was touring Russia, which is something I've always wanted to do, and found some beautiful women who didn't know who I was, had never heard of me, didn't know a blitz from a backfield in motion, liked me just for myself, that would be different. Then I could trust her. Then I could do some serious wining and dining. "More borscht, boubala?"

My idea of the perfect evening is to have a limousine take me and my lady to a restaurant we've rented all to ourselves. Then we have the chef make whatever we want. "Let's see, Pierre. Tonight I can't decide if I'm in the mood for fettucini or Chinese food. You decide." And then we'd go to a play. I'm crazy about plays. Then we'd go back home, turn on the hot tub, have the candles going, a fire blazing, a little Terence Trent D'Arby on the stereo, and . . . sorry, I've got to go take a cold shower.

But I do like to look. I like especially to look at somebody like Raquel Welch's daughter. Raquel herself is getting a little ancient for me, but her genes do pretty nicely in her daughter. Kathleen Turner is a fox. I'd hop down Park Avenue naked on one foot for a date with her. After I taped "Late Night with David Letterman" during my junior season, I went out to dinner with a friend of mine and his friend happened to be with her and some other guy. We didn't say much to each other, but I thought she was beautiful. Cybill Shepherd is not beautiful. I would let Debbie Gibson touch me. Gloria Estefan from Miami Sound Machine is sexy as hell. Madonna I like because she does her own thing. She's nice-looking and she's got a hard body, as the whole world has seen by now. But she's probably got the intellect of a coffee table.

What else . . . I hate smokers. I hate old people with driver's licenses who can't drive. If I was President, I'd make anybody with blue hair and a driver's license move to Oregon. Stick 'em all in one state. That's where a lot of 'em are anyway. Then you could have yellow lights that are two minutes long so they could get through them and green lights that are fifteen minutes long so they have time to see them, put their foot on the gas pedal, and actually get through them.

I hate it when people drive down the highway picking their nose; trophy digging. I hate it when motorcycles take up an entire parking spot. Anytime I see a motorcycle taking up a spot I want to park in, I get out and move it.

And sometimes I hate being famous.

I realize I have no call to complain about being famous, since I brought all this fame on myself. I wanted to be famous. I wanted to be different . . . better, I guess. I thrive on the spotlight. Always have. So I'm not complaining about signing autographs or being recognized or having people come up to talk to me or not being able to go to a restaurant or a movie or the mall like normal people. I asked for it all.

I just never figured on there being so many total assholes in the world. I never counted on so many people growing up in an Amana refrigerator somewhere and never learning any manners. I never knew how many people in this country have never heard of soap. It's like I'd love to tell half the people I meet, "A tube of toothpaste and a Reach toothbrush would do you a world of good, home boy."

I never figured I'd have people coming up to me in the john while I'm standing there taking a leak and wanting to shake my hand. Seriously.

Some guy will come up while I'm relieving myself and say, "Boz, I just want to shake your hand." And he'll put his hand out.

"You're *surrrrrre* about this?" I'll say. "This is a desire you want fulfilled *right now*?"

Or a guy will come up while I'm standing there and put his hand on my shoulder and say, "So, Boz, what's up?"

"Oh, nothing much. I always come into little rooms like this and stand facing the wall for no reason at all. What's up with you? Lobotomy come out all right?"

I don't know what it is with people. It's like they don't think of me as a person. They think of me as some sort of museum piece they can just come up and rub. I've had people snatch the fork out of my mouth at dinner and say, "I know you hate to be bothered, but . . ."

Like I'm supposed to say, "Oh yes, but that's just by the *public*. You're not the public. You're special. You probably want something much different. Like an autograph for your next-door neighbor's manicurist's son. *Welllll*, by all means, just take the goddamn thirty-dollar lobster out of my mouth, interrupt my friend who was talking about his coming triple-bypass operation, put a pen in my hand, and let's get right to it."

Or the people who come right up in the middle of lunch at a restaurant and sit right down. They don't *ask* to sit down. They don't say please. They just sit down. And then they say something like "Boz, lemme fly a couple questions off ya. Whadju think of the way Kansas City was runnin' that option pass at you? Now, the way I see it . . ."

I mean, can you imagine him doing that to anybody else's table? "So, Mr. and Mrs. Fitzelstine, lemme ask you a few questions. I noticed you haven't done much with your lawn this summer. Now, I think you oughta . . ." They'd lock him in the wine cellar until the morning.

And then you try to politely get rid of the guy and he doesn't get the message, so you *give* him the damn message and he gets all bent out of shape.

"Well, I guess you're just like they say."

"No, I'm worse than they say. And if you don't get out of my face, you're about to find out why."

But I always sit there, like a moron, and listen to their whole spiel or sign what they wanted signed. I can remember only one time when I didn't. We were in Pittsburgh and this guy came up to our table while we were eating—he literally grabbed my arm while I was lifting my fork to my mouth—and he said, "I promised myself I'd never do this to a celebrity ever since the time I saw Franco Harris bothered to death at a restaurant one night. But when I saw you, Boz, I just had to come over and ask you to sign this."

I sat there for a second and then I said, "Nope."

"Nope what?"

"Nope, I won't sign it."

"Why not?" he said.

"Because you said you promised yourself you'd never do this and I can't be responsible for how terrible you'll feel about yourself in the morning. Just couldn't do it to you.''

He just walked away, shocked. What could he say?

One time a guy came up to me in a bar and said, ''I'd really like to get your autograph. My son thinks you're great . . .''

So I started to sign and then he said, ''. . . but I think you're an asshole.''

The nerve. I just ripped the thing up. If you're going to ask me for an autograph, at least pretend you like me.

I don't see why everybody wants to get their two cents in with me in the first place. Why does everybody have to let me know what they think about me, my clothes, my football ability, the space race, the nuclear age, and every other friggin' thing? Check out my driver's license. It does not say: HARRIS POLL TAKER.

I'll sign autographs until the last guy leaves the place if I have to, but I have no idea what people do with the stuff. I've signed some weird stuff—matchbook covers, Chinet plates, underwear, car doors. You name it, I've signed it. I think most people put the little scraps of paper in the bottom of their purse or their pocket and wait for some scary piece of gum to get old and use it to wad the stuff up.

One time I was getting out of a limousine and a lady came up to me and asked me to sign her breast. It wasn't the first time it's happened either. Some guys might think that sounds like fun, but let me tell you, there are a whole lot more breasts in this world you'd rather *not* see than ones you would. She was begging me to do it and her boyfriend was standing behind her with this *Deliverance* kind of look on his face and he's saying, "*Yeaaaah, mannnn*. Do it, dude. She'll get off on it." What kind of scumbag is this? The guy wants another guy to be handling his girlfriend's hooter? But I didn't do it. The way I look at it, if this lady will whip it out at an airport for an autograph, no telling where the thing has been.

What really hacks me off is when people come up and say, "Would you please sign this? My mother's *dying* and she really wants your autograph." Right. I can just see her on her deathbed, lying there, saying, "Oh, son, I just have one last request. Go seek out Brian Bosworth and get his autograph." I mean, if the woman is dying, what the hell is she gonna do with it anyway?

I only have a few autograph rules. I never do it during a meal and I won't write some bull that I don't know to be true. "To my best friend and spiritual adviser, Reginald." Nuh-uh. Or "Dear Lucinda, thanks for a *great* night." That's the kind of junk that gets you in trouble. I've got enough people going around pretending to be me as it is.

That happened all the time in Norman. I'd see my girlfriend and right away I'd have to start defending myself. "Cathy Jo said she saw you out with some blonde bimbette at Confetti's last night at two A.M. I thought you were studying!"

And of course, I'd have to say, "I swear that wasn't me!" And it'd be very hard to believe me. There were guys going around, big guys with blond haircuts exactly like mine, telling girls they were me. Most of the bartenders knew me at Confetti's— this big dance club in Oklahoma City—and one night when I went in there one of 'em called me over and said, "That guy is here tonight who says he's you. Right over there."

He was talking to these three girls, big-timing it and talking about Oklahoma football. "Oh yeah, we were so far ahead, I was out by halftime . . ." He looked a *lot* like me, actually. Colors in his hair and everything. It was almost scary.

So I said, "Hey, man, what's up?"

And he started to say, "Oh, nothin' much . . ." and then he turned around and saw who it was and he got all nervous and started stammering. And he walked off and the girls looked at me and said, "Who are you?"

"Uh, my name's Jeff."

I mean, I didn't want to ruin the guy's *whole* evening.

But it turned out I should've turned his face into plasma because later he went down to South Padre Island and all my friends came back and told me he was telling people he was me and creating all kinds of hell. If I'm going to get thrown in jail, I'd at least like to have the fun that goes with it.

This junk is already starting to happen in Seattle. A bunch of times already I've been at some bar, throwing down some malted beverages, and some girl will come up pissed off at me, some girl I'd never met before and she'll say, "I can't *believe* you came back here after what you said to me last night. You were so *rude*."

"Honey, I've never even *seen* you before."

I wonder what I did?

I'm just waiting for one of these times when the police come knocking on my door.

"Come with us," they'll say.

"Why?"

"You just robbed a 7-Eleven."

"Really? How much did I get?"

"$37.50 and six bags of Reese's Pieces."

But until I can buy my own island and decide who I want to let on it and who I don't, I have to deal with life in a fishbowl, as they say. I used to get a real kick out of it, but it's done too much to screw up my life for me to enjoy it anymore. I can't even go out like a regular human being. I don't *dare* go to a movie. I went to a Celtics-Sonics game one night my rookie year and I think I saw one basket the whole time. The rest of the time I was just sitting there, signing. I might as well have signed. All the people were blocking my view.

I've tried disguises and weird sunglasses, but nothing works. I know it's not my hair because I've worn hats and they still recognize me. I tried growing a goatee, but I looked like Charles Manson.

So I just adjust. If I go out for dinner at all, I go at about ten or eleven at night. If I shop, I call the store just before closing and ask them if it's all right if I come in and they can close the gates and I can shop in relative peace. They're always nice about it.

After Oklahoma games it got to where I was signing autographs for two hours until my hand would start to cramp up. So I had to take drastic measures: an escape route. From the locker room I'd go up the top ramp, sneak across the street, run over to somebody's dorm room to hide out for about an hour, then out the back way. Then I'd run to my car and floor it to get away. I swear, I've been in some car chases *Miami Vice* hasn't even thought of yet. I'd be doing eighty-five in my Corvette and some fan would be doing eighty-five right behind me in some Ford Fairlane. They'd have that Fairlane going like a damn Porsche 911. They'd be breaking the law just like I would. I'd run lights, stop signs, use the shoulder, and so would they. They'd follow me all the way to the house. I'd drive up, open the garage door, pull my car in, and two seconds later there'd be a knock at the door, asking me to sign. Christ, I should ask for their autograph. "Aren't you Richard Petty?"

One of the worst things about being famous is when someone is being a total asshole to you, wants to fight you, is begging to get some free dental work done, you can't do it. Like the time I was in this pool place in Dallas with Toy and Troy, my two childhood buddies. I started to kick this one guy's ass who was asking for it and then I stopped and said to myself, "I can't do this." So I tagged off to Toy and Troy and they did it for me.

It's amazing to me how many guys want to fight me. Why they'd want to fight an NFL linebacker I have no idea, but they do. I suppose it's because they know if I touch them my picture will show up in the paper beating the hell out of some electrician and they can sue. What I plan on doing, though, some-day, is having a couple bodyguards with me, but not near me. Always around but not so anybody would notice. Anybody that wants to fight I just say, "Sorry, I can't. But these fellas here might be will-ing to assist you." Then I give these two animals the word. "Crocodile, Boot Face, go introduce yourself to the guy in the Johnny Miller K-mart sport jacket."

All right, already. Enough bitching. Fame has its kicks. Fame can be a riot. Like how many guys have the President drop their name into casual conversation? President Reagan was coming through Norman once and he said, "I know Norman is famous for oil wells and Bosworth. This is the land of Boz." I swear. It was in the paper. Stop by anytime, Ronnie.

Or like the time my agent, Gary Wichard, and I were in the L.A. airport. We were waiting to use the phone and Gary says, "Look, it's Bob Dylan."

"Who the hell is Bob Dylan?"

That freaked Gary out. *"You don't know who Bob Dylan is?"*

Just then Dylan gets off the phone and says, "Hey, Boz," and introduces himself. I'd never heard of him, but I guess he'd heard of me. After that I bought a few of his albums and now I listen to his music. I like it. Small world.

And how many guys have done "The Tonight Show," "Late Night with David Letterman," all the morning network shows, and all the rest? Not bad for a kid from MacArthur High.

And how many guys have had Donald Trump send a limousine for them at the airport and then put them up in one of his suites at the Trump Tower. "Nice digs you got here, Don." That was just before the Holmes–Tyson fight, which we saw. Trump took us to a birthday party for Muhammad Ali the night before the fight. Everybody at that party looked like they'd just bought a Mr. T starter set, wearing all sorts of big fat gold chains. Nobody's wearing shirts either, just chains. I guess they thought that looked good, but I thought it looked horseshit. What sense does it make to have a medallion the size of a Mercedes emblem hanging around your neck? What are you gonna wear next? Chevrolet?

I talked to Ali, but I couldn't understand a word he said. Then Don King, the fight promoter (would I say anything about his hair?) came over and started talking for him. Don King is bad news. He's the kind of guy who, as soon as somebody famous comes up and starts talking to him, gets real loud so everybody will look.

That was the same night I met Lou Albano, the pro wrestler, who sweated all over me. Thanks, Lou. I wanted to take a shower right then. As you may have figured out, I'm a fanatic about being clean. I take four showers a day, no joke. One when I get up. One before I work out. One after I work out. And one before I go to bed. I know it's weird to take one before you work out, but I like to sweat clean. And some people might not take one before you go to bed, but I like to sleep clean too.

Or maybe it's just because I love taking showers. I'll sit in the shower for forty-five minutes at a time. If the shower is big enough, I'll take a chair in there—a plastic or a metal chair—and just sit in there and let the water hit me. *Sports Illustrated* shot me bare-ass naked sitting in a chair in a shower in the OU locker room. I got a lot of reaction off that. Marriage proposals from women. Some proposals from some really strange men too. But that was the funnest shoot I've ever had. "Okay, Brian. Just sit there in the shower. Fine, fine." I'll sit in a shower for a month if you want me to. In my dream house, I'm going to have a shower with four nozzles, so the water hits you from all sides. I'll have a chaise lounge in there, built in, comfortable, and I'll just sleep in there for hours at a time. Maybe get a waterproof phone in case anybody needs me.

I like to look good. Always wear my shades. I wear these blue wraparounds called Gargoyles, which is a prototype of the kind we're going to make with my line of young men's clothes called 44 Blues. That's another reason I was so pissed about Pete Rozelle making me wear 55. We already have an entire line of clothes ready to go out under the name 44 Blues. What are we going to do, change all those tags to say 55 Blues? Bald son of a bitch is costing me some serious money.

People ask my why I wear my shades during interviews. Well, it's because most of the time they have that big damn bright light streaming right in your eyes. Plus, with the shades on, I don't have to look at anything. Don't have to look at the camera or Brent or anybody. I hate looking at the camera because they usually have somebody fat and disgusting sitting behind the camera with one eye open looking like a pirate. Besides, the shades keep me from revealing too much of myself.

I've got a serious jones for clothes. I must have twenty pairs of jeans. I wear mostly black. Makes you look ominous. The Raiders sent me this one sweatshirt: REAL MEN WEAR BLACK. I wear it all the time. That's my attitude. I guess I'm into clothes so much because I used to be a real Gomer in high school. Lots of polyester, lots of blends, Levi's that zip up, golf shirts your dad would wear. I looked like Lumpy Rutherford.

A lot of guys on the Seahawks still wear that kind of stuff, the offensive linemen especially. All offensive linemen have Plumber's Butt. That's when the plumber comes over to your house and bends over to fix the sink and the crack of his ass comes about four inches out of his pants. That's Plumber's Butt. Linemen are hopeless. They wear shirt-pant combos that look like something they got out of a box of Duz.

My buddy and fellow rookie linebacker Dave Wyman will admit he was hurting in the style department when he first got to Seattle. I don't know what his problem was. He came from Stanford. There's some hip stuff in Stanford. But he was wearing tablecloths for shirts, real Stretcho-matic-type plaid stuff. And I said to him, "Damn, what are you, a lumberjack?"

Besides him and a few other guys on the team— Sam Merriman, Keith Butler, Greg Gaines, and a few more—I don't hang with football players very much in Seattle. In the pros, all they want to do is talk shop, bitch about this coach or that coach. "He hates me." Stuff like that. I'd just as soon divorce myself from that. Or they'll want to watch sports on TV. I never watch sports on TV, unless it's "Monday Night Football" and we're playing one of the two teams later that year. Or they always want to go hunting. Some sport. "Okay, you're a moose. Now you run and I'll try to shoot your ass dead with this high-powered rifle. Fun, eh?" Now I'm going to hang his head on my wall? Nah.

Mostly I keep to my own friends and listen to my music. I love music and I love it loud. I don't believe anybody on Earth likes their music any louder than I do. I spent about $7,000 getting my car stereo system just the way I wanted it. Anybody that gets in there with me has to sign a release saying they won't sue for hearing aids. It's got nine speakers and a 1,000-watt amplifier. One of the speakers is fifteen inches around by itself. I had it so loud once that it drained the battery—the biggest battery Delco makes—and the car was *running*. That's loud.

Almost as loud as one of Wyman's shirts.

CHAPTER
10

Miami Twice

Nineteen hundred and eighty-six, the Year of our Lord, was one of the greatest years of my life and one of the worst years of my life.

I won the Dick Butkus Award as the best linebacker in the nation for the second year in a row. I got suspended from the Orange Bowl for using steroids. I finished fourth in the country for the Heisman Trophy. I had to write two public apology letters, neither of which I meant. I was named All-American for the third year in a row. We lost to Miami. I appeared on the cover of *Sports Illustrated* as the man to watch for the coming season. I appeared on the cover of *Sports Illustrated* under the steroid headline: BOZ FLUNKS OUT. Switzer named me as one of the three greatest Oklahoma players in history—along with Billy Sims and Lee Roy Selmon. Switzer kicked me off the team. Nice year.

It was a year that was just plain-ass out of control. Everything about it was out of control. My fame, the press, the fans, my life, Norman, everything. I remember one day, before our season opener with UCLA in Norman, I started out doing a cover shot for some campus magazine. Then I did an interview for them. Then I talked to a bunch of out-of-town writers from Los Angeles and San Francisco. Then

I posed for a picture for *Time*. Then I had to speak to a group of disabled kids from around the state. Then I did a thing for CBS. Then I did an interview for *Sooners Illustrated*. Somehow in there I was supposed to go to class, study, go to practice, watch film, and carry on a normal social life. And the NCAA likes to call us students first, athletes second.

I didn't know how to say no and I was driving me and everybody who had to deal with me crazy. Pat Hanlon, my main man in the sports publicity department, once told me he spent more time outside of classrooms waiting for me to get out so he could take me to my next interview than he spent in classrooms when *he* was going to school.

By the end of that year my mind was just numb. I had wilted. I had dealt with so many people, had done so many interviews, had posed for so many pictures, had signed so many autographs, had dealt with so many problems that I almost flipped out. I was written up in everything from *The Wall Street Journal* to *Interview* magazine. I guess Andy Warhol thought I was his kind of guy. One guy came all the way from London to interview me. Sporting chap, actually. I don't know why he came, though. Compared to some of the haircuts I've seen in London, I must look like an undertaker.

I had so many requests for autographs that the football office would order twenty-five hundred pictures of me a month. Then, when I'd go on a trip somewhere, Sheryl, the football secretary, would give me a stack of three hundred and fifty pictures to sign, with the names of the persons I was supposed to sign them to. I'd fly from Oklahoma City to Dallas and Dallas to New York, signing pictures the whole way. They ought to donate my right hand to the Smithsonian.

I should've known things were out of control the day they unveiled our new national championship sign, 1985, on the scoreboard. There were three thousand people there. I think the thing started at two and I was still there signing autographs at seven o'clock that night.

From there began one of the wildest years in my life, maybe *the* wildest year. Some things were a kick to do. Like I did the "Late Night with David Letterman" show in January. For such a hilarious guy, Letterman sure is depressed a lot. The whole time before the show he looked like he'd just lost everything in the stock market. He's always worrying about his hair too. So, on the show, when he asked me what I was going to do next with my hair, I said, "Well, Dave, I might go with the Letterman cut."

I went to all those preseason All-American deals. Like *Playboy* brought all of us down to the Bal Harbour Hotel in Miami for three days to shoot one picture. And they tell you, "Order whatever you want while you're here. It's on us."

That's a tactical blunder. One night we were all up in one of the guy's rooms ordering enough room service stuff to feed Cuba. I personally ordered three entrees and two desserts and a chef's salad. Some of the other guys ordered a bunch of stuff too and then, just as I was about to hang up with the guy from down there, somebody says, "Hey, Boz, let's try a little of this *kahn-yak* stuff."

"What's *kahn-yak*?" I said. I'd never heard of cognac in my life.

"I dunno," the guy says, "but I hear it's good."

So I tell the guy, "And you better send up about five bottles of this *kahn-yak* stuff."

The bill was $650 for that one meal and the cognac alone was $90 a bottle. I think we drank one sip each and spit it out. We were real class acts back then.

Those things are free-for-alls, and I do mean *free*. Guys went down to the gift shop and signed for stuff you wouldn't believe. They were getting shorts and shoes and stuffed animals and clocks and stupid things they'd never use, like ashtrays and little porcelain figures. Just my luck, by the time I found out about it, *Playboy* cut it off.

One time at the Kodak thing in Los Angeles I got so drunk I was taking coins out of the fountain to pay our bar tab. And then when I got tired of doing that, I was just reaching up and snagging drinks off the trays of passing cocktail waitresses. She'd arrive at her table and go, "Hmmmm. I sure am forgetful tonight. I keep forgetting drinks."

That was the trip when I was at this lobster restaurant and the waiter asked me what I wanted and I said, "The lobster."

"Which entree of lobster, sir?"

"The lobster," I said.

"Yes, sir. But we have five lobster entrees on the menu, sir."

"Right," I said, and I ate 'em all.

That's like the time I was really hungry when we went into this restaurant in Norman and this friend of mine was buying, so when the waiter came up to me and asked what I wanted, I said, "Page three." Ate all that too.

The only problem with the Kodak deal is that you have to go do the Bob Hope All-American show. I don't know how a guy thinks he can come in and do his own show with one day of rehearsal, but that's how he does it. He doesn't even *pretend* he's got them memorized. He just stares right at the card. The guy was great once, but he's *way* past getting the gold watch stage now. I hope when my time comes, I'll know when to quit.

The best part of those All-American things, though, is meeting the players. I became pretty good friends with Vinny Testaverde that year. I like Vinny because he likes to win. He'll do anything to win. And he's got a knack for doing the right thing at the right time. We'd be better friends, though, if the son of a bitch would give me back my Heisman.

This seemed like the year when the world discovered The Boz, and everybody wanted a piece of him. Especially road crowds. They wanted a piece of my cranium. The crowds that year—and in my first NFL year—seemed to just go bonkers. Everyone that bought a ticket all seemed to have the same mission in life: rag on me.

What kills me about fans is they scream all this stuff at me and act real cocky about it, like they're the first ones to think of it. Like "What is a Boz worth? Absolutely nothing!" Or "Your name ought to be Bozo, not Boz!" Yuck yuck. There's not a thing in the world you can say to me that I haven't heard. It's all reruns, pal.

But what's funny is they'll say it from behind a fence. So I make a quick little move their way and holler something at them like "*Aaaaargh*, shit-head!" They about jump into the mezzanine. I don't know why they're so scared. There's a fence between us. They can say anything they want to. What am I going to do, scale the fence five minutes before kickoff?

I learned one trick that year: always leave your helmet on. Once you've had bottles and cans and snowballs and oranges and rocks and coins and everything else thrown at you, you realize the place you need your helmet the most is on the sideline. And I always get a good spraying from the drunks waiting by the tunnel. Doesn't matter if I haven't had a drink all day, by the time I get through that tunnel, listening to all their words of wisdom, I'd be lucky to pass a sobriety test.

I love it when I get *my* chance to dog somebody else. Like the time we went to an OU-Texas baseball game and sat right behind the Texas dugout. We were beating the face off the Shorthorns, 15–2, and I'm calling their coach "Bacon Head" because he's been out in the sun all his life and the back of his neck is so wrinkled. All of a sudden one of their players hollers out, "Hey, Boz! How'd your girlfriend know where we were staying last night?"

I was over that dugout fence in a flash. I was going to pull the guy's spleen out by way of his ear. You can say anything you want about me, but rag on my mother or my girlfriend and my brain synapses start to fry. I got in one good right hand on somebody, I don't even know if it was the guy who said it in the first place—and they all jumped me and my friends jumped them and it was a regular Wrestlemania 3. They had to postpone the game until they could get us the hell out of the ballpark.

But after a while, having *so* many people wanting

to get to you—whether to hug you or slug you—it starts to warp your brain. It was definitely getting a little scary. In Miami—and later at Mile High Stadium in Denver for the Broncos game—I had to have cops walk me in and out. And sometimes that wouldn't even help. When the game ended, I'd try sprinting to the tunnel. But there was usually two or three hundred fans over the wall by then and most of 'em want my ass. They'd start grabbing me, pulling on my jersey, my towel, my belt. Anything they can get their hands on. And these are people that *like* me. You start to feel like a half-priced purse at a women's clearance sale.

It gets scary, especially when you get four or five people coming up from behind you, people you don't see. They're patting you on the back, but how do you know when the next pat will have a knife in it? That's why I never go out by myself anymore—anywhere. I always need somebody to watch me. And I always have whoever I'm with watching my backside. Either that or I'll stand against a wall, so I've got my back protected. There's just too many weirdos out there.

I started to get so paranoid about people that year that I began carrying a gun in my car. I had a .357 Magnum with a six-inch barrel under my seat. Sometimes I'd even carry it on me. A friend of mine bought it for me. I got it because I had people trying to break into my house. It was starting to be common knowledge in Norman by then where I lived and I was getting a lot of weird things happening to me. I walked up to my house one day and the front door was wide open. And when I got inside, there was a chair thrown through the window. After that I got my Doberman, Raider, and my gun.

I've only used it—the gun—once. It was about two in the morning one night and Raider was prancing around the house like she had rabies. I was stark naked. "Raider, what's wrong with you?" All of a sudden my car alarm went off. I opened the door and let Raider out, then I heard a car take off. I grabbed a towel and my gun. I got outside in time to see this car flying down the street, fifty yards from me. So I just fired a shot right at the car. Don't know if I hit anything or what, but I sure as hell scared whoever it was.

That's when I realized it was time to get the hell out of Norman. There I was, walking back to my house in a towel with a smoking gun on my shoulder, cussing like a drunken sailor. And just then a neighbor looked out her window—an old lady—and saw me and I'll never forget the expression on her face. She probably figured I was Sheriff Matt Dillon gone totally insane. That town was just getting too damn small for me.

All I had to do was get through one last season and I knew I was gone. Switzer may not have known I was going to jump to the pros a year early. The press may not have known it. But I did.

It was a strange season, too. We were the number one ranked team in the country that year and we wanted to win the national championship again. We knew that the whole season was one game—Miami—and we weren't very sure we could win that one game. I mean, we had almost the same team back, with the exception of losing Mr. Nose Guard, Cas-

illas. B.F.D. Everybody said that without Casillas
I was going to disappear. Said that Casillas took all
the heat off of me. That turned out to be bullshit. I
played better without his big ass in there than I did
with him.

That whole year we worked on Miami stuff whenever we could. In the spring. In the summer. When
we were getting ready to play Minnesota, we devoted three days to them and the other two to Miami.
We *wanted* Miami bad. They'd come to our backyard
the year before and stolen our girlfriends. The problem was, the game was in Miami and we all knew
that a wishbone team was going to have a bitch of a
time beating the fast defensive team on grass.

But we weren't worried—yet. We were supposed
to be worrying about UCLA, which came in at number four in the country. They looked like a hundred
and four to me. I told a reporter before the game
that I thought they looked like they played girls'
football. I was wrong. Girls play better football than
UCLA played that day. We blew them away, 38–3.
Their quarterback, Matt Stevens, either had no idea
how to wear a uniform or was playing in his mother's
girdle. Only one butt to a pair of pants, please. And
he threw *worse* than his mother. I was screaming at
their offensive linemen, "Hit us . . . HIT US!!" All
they were doing was crawling along the ground, div-
ing at our legs.

"Get your big ass up and hit one of us!"

They didn't follow instructions very well.

After the game at the press conference—I was
having to hold a press conference once during the
week and once after every game now—I said, "Well,
last year we opened with a semi-doormat in Min-

nesota. This year we opened with a legitimate doormat.''

I thought it was a good line. Not to mention it was the truth. The next thing I know Switzer is calling me into his office. Our Chief of Chafe, the Dishonorable Frank E. Horton, had taken offense to my remark.

"Horton is *pissed*," Switzer said.

"What about?" I said innocently.

"You know what about. He wants you to write an apology letter. He says you slandered a fine university."

"I didn't slander the university," I said. "I slandered the football team. There's a big difference. Besides, they deserved it. Didn't you think they sucked?"

"Yeah, but that's not the point."

Horton got his apology letter. I didn't even read it. I have no idea who wrote it. I just read about it in the paper the next day. Put it this way, anytime in my life you've seen my name at the bottom of an apology letter, you can bet your last stick of beef jerky I didn't write it. The only reason I did it was for my teammates. I didn't want Horton to start coming down on us and hurting the team.

The next week we kicked The Original Doormat, Minnesota, 63–0. They'd lost Lou Holtz just before the season and they were pitiful. I played about a quarter and a half. My jock didn't even get wet. By the second quarter, I was already thinking about our next game: Miami.

Everybody in the country knew the winner would have a damn good chance to be the national champion. Not only that, but they were saying it was a game to decide the Heisman between me and Vinny. It was a thrilling week, and the whole time Switzer was walking around, saying, "Men, they don't have the answer. We're going to *shock* their ass!" He kept saying that, and the *shock* part kept getting a little louder and longer every time. "They don't have the answer, men, I'm tellin' you. We're going to *shock* their ass!" And he'd get more and more pumped up every time he'd say it.

Us too. I wore army fatigues on the plane down there, just to show that this meant war. I guess the Miami fans had the same thing in mind. When I got to the stadium, they're wearing real subtle T-shirts like F__ THE BOZ. And they're burning me in effigy up in the balcony. How smart is that? They've got a full stadium and they're hanging something off a rope and setting it on fire. I guess it makes them feel like they're back home in Liberty City. I was hoping that my likeness would fall down on the crowd and burn a few 'Canes to cinders. No such luck.

That game was one of the most intense, loud, feverish things I've ever been involved in. I don't think I've ever been more pumped up before a game. Everybody was. When they were getting ready to toss the coin, both benches were clear out to the hashmarks, screaming obscenities at each other. One guy on my team was just flatout calling Highsmith "a nigger." Just kept screaming that at him. And this guy's best friend is a black guy. We were all just losing it.

I remember looking over at the refs. They were scared to death. They were starting to realize that they'd been thrown in with a pen full of wild animals and there was no way out. The tension level was ungodly high.

Unfortunately, we had to play the game. We got our ass kicked. Guys were walking around on the sidelines at the end going, ''Well, we really *shocked* their ass, didn't we?''

As things turned out, *we* didn't have the answer. We had a great game plan—full of blitzes and stunts—and we didn't use a damn one of them. Don't ask my why. I know there are certain times when you can't blitz, but we never blitzed. Just like we didn't blitz the year before against them. We finally started blitzing in the fourth quarter and I got a sack on Vinny, but by then it was way too late. Vinny had already folded, stapled, and mutilated us with four touchdown passes. Our offense couldn't tie their shoes against Miami's defense. We got kicked, 28–16.

I had twenty-two tackles, but I felt like death. Once I got into the locker room, my back and my kidneys started cramping up. I was so dehydrated that I wasn't even sweating anymore. I started shaking and I was cold as ice. They stuck a bunch of IVs in me and eventually I was all right. But I lost about fifteen pounds that game. Plus the national championship. Plus the Heisman Trophy.

At least I gave everything I had that day. I'd tried to be all over the field. I got in a lot of fights. I didn't like a few of their guys because I could tell they were all coked up. Their eyes were big as spaghetti plates. I'm not lecturing people about coke, but if they want to do it, do it after the game. I asked Vinny about it later on in the year and he said that yeah, a few of their guys always got coked up for games. I don't think he liked it much either.

On that flight home we were so depressed we were drinking in the back like crazy. College players aren't supposed to have liquor, but we'd always sneak a few bottles into our carry-ons and then mix it with the sodas the stewardi would give us. We were tossing it down when all of a sudden Coach Selmon walks back from first-class. Everybody likes Coach Selmon. He's cool about things. He must be the most laid-back coach ever. He was talking to us and then he smelled it.

"Okay, give it to me," he said. "Whoever has it, just give it to me. I don't want to know who it is."

Well, at this point in the evening I was past caring, so I held the bottle up and said, "Okay, Coach, but do you mind if I at least go ahead and pour myself a fresh one?"

He didn't seem amused. But it *was* a brand-new bottle. He took it back with him up in first-class and I'm sure he and Switzer and all the coaches drank it. They were as depressed as we were.

The rest of the season was just a bunch of Saturdays spent beating the ectoplasm out of teams and then hoping to hear that Miami had lost. They never did—until it was too late.

We just massacred people. Kansas State and their putrid helmets, 56–10. Texas, 47–12. (Afterward, a reporter asked me if I'd ever imagined I'd see the day when Texas would lose by thirty-five points to OU and I said, "I never imagined, I only just hoped. You pray for things like that." I guess Horton never got his paper the next day because I didn't have to write any letters.) Oklahoma State, 19–0. Iowa State,

38–0. Kansas (which got a whopping minus fifty-seven yards rushing in a game that was so fascinating that I spent most of the second half getting my picture taken with their cheerleaders), 64–3. Missouri, 77–0. And Colorado, 28–0 (in which I waved hello to all my Buffalo fans with my middle finger and started pitching the oranges they had thrown at me back at them).

That's four shutouts, five games without allowing a touchdown, and the honor of being the number-one-ranked offense *and* defense in the country. All of which didn't mean diddly. Miami still hadn't lost and we were realizing our chances for the national mpionship were zip, especially since Penn State was undefeated too. Penn State was setting up a game with Miami in the Fiesta Bowl.

So all that was left for us to do was beat Nebraska and go back to the Orange Bowl. But you know what? None of us *wanted* to go back to the Orange Bowl. We were *sick* of going back to the Orange Bowl. We'd been there the last two years straight. It was about as appetizing as dorm food. Guys were walking around before the Nebraska game, saying, "Damn, man! I want to go someplace *new*."

But it's funny. As soon as we got on that field, we all made up our minds that we wanted to go back to the Orange Bowl. Because the Orange Bowl isn't so much a place as a trophy, and we we wanted that trophy. We came back from being down 17–7 in the fourth quarter and won, 20–17, partly because of the best tight end in the game, Keith, and partly because our defense at the end was tighter than Michael Jackson's new face. That felt good. Three years at Oklahoma and three times we kicked Nebraska's ass, which isn't easy. Those were damn tough Nebraska teams.

We were headed to the Orange Bowl, our winter home, to play 9–2 Arkansas, not the most exciting trip in the world, but better than looking at your jersey and having it say TEXAS. At least we could hit that beach again and look at those topless women.

Personally, I knew my Heisman was history by then. Actually, I always figured it was history. I only cared about the Butkus Award because I thought the panel of voters they had were knowledgeable—twenty guys from around the country who specialized in college football. The Heisman? Christ, they gave the Heisman to Doug (If I Could Only Be Five-Foot-Six) Flutie. Who can take the award seriously after that? It's like "Wait a minute. Doug Flutie's name is on this trophy. Here. Take it back." Besides, they usually give the thing out after two or three games anyway. That's what they did with Tim Brown. It was his maybe even before that. He won it by virtue of a great summer of running routes in his shorts.

I knew from the beginning that I didn't have a chance to win that Heisman. I don't know if a defensive player will ever win under the system they have now. For one thing, all they have is a bunch of old farts who vote on the thing. Half of the old farts hate me because they're old and the other half don't know who anybody is because their newspaper got them on the voting list a hundred years ago and they don't even watch college football now. A lot of them don't ever turn their ballots back in. And those that do watch only what happens on the offensive side of the ball. Hell, all they *watch* is the ball. They have no idea what I'm doing—whether I'm in the right place, what I did to get to the carrier, whether I had my man covered or not. There's no way they're even 10 percent knowledgeable enough to make the Heisman a realistic contest.

And even if I had been far and away the best choice, the voters still wouldn't do it because I played defense. "What'd you say, man? This is the *Heisman* we're talking about here. Don't you see the football in his hand? Don't no defensive player carry no football in his hand."

Not that I didn't think Vinny was a good choice. He had a great year. Besides, in the one game when we went head-to-head, his team won. He played great that day, but I thought I played pretty damn well too. But it was over after that.

The only thing I liked about being up for the Heisman was that you got a free trip to New York. I love New York. My kind of place. People just go, "Hey! Get outta my way already!" They don't mean it personally or anything. They're just telling you that you're in their way and it's no big deal. In Seattle you say something like that and you're under arrest. It's like you stole their watch or something. Seattle people take things so personally. New Yorkers are cool about it. Every sentence they say has to have the word "f__" in it. It's the law.

They bring you to New York for a big dinner before the ceremony. You're supposed to be nervous about it until the very moment when the joker from Price-Waterhouse or wherever brings out the envelope and they announce it. In fact, the photographers wanted to shoot all five of us—one by one, holding the trophy, just to build the tension.

So I said, "Wait a minute. Let me check. Hey, Vinny, do you mind if we get our picture taken with your trophy?"

The only disappointment I had in not winning the thing is that I would have given it to my dad for all that he did for me. That would have really made him proud. Oh well, screw it. I had awards he could be proud of. I became the first player in OU history to start thirty-six consecutive games over a three-year period, which meant I never let down anybody that counted on me. We were 31–4–1 and won three Big Eight titles and a national championship.

But it's funny about the Heisman. The King used that as a selling point to try to get me back for my senior year.

"Look," Switzer said to me one day. "We're going to put together a whole program for you to win the Heisman next year. We'll make sure you have everything you need to win the thing. We'll put that trophy right next to Billy's [Sims] and Steve's [Owens] and make it a great year for you."

"Thanks, Coach," I said. "But no thanks."

There wasn't anything else he could offer. I didn't need any money. I was probably making almost as much money as he was that year.

Besides, he had to know I was leaving. I was taking eighteen credits that last semester. You'd have to be out of your damn mind to take eighteen credits if you had a whole year left to get it done. He knew it was coming. I think he'd known for two years. My parents knew too, so they came to every game—home and away—which isn't cheap. That's a real highlight in my life, the fact that they were proud enough of me to do that.

The only thing I wanted was the hole card. It was what I had wanted since I came to OU my freshman year. I wanted to be able to say to the NFL, ''Look, I might jump early and I might not. It depends on who takes me.'' That way I knew I could work a deal to play in a city I wanted for the money I wanted.

I had all the leverage in the world. I had Pete Rozelle's bald head by the ears. I was all set.

Until three o'clock on the afternoon of December 17, 1986.

That's when they really *shocked* my ass.

CHAPTER
11

Hello, Moscow

One of the things we'd do during practice at Oklahoma was take bets on when our man Nuke would die.

"I'll bet he goes today," I'd say.

"Ten-to-one says he doesn't," somebody else would say.

"How much?"

"Five bucks."

Nuke was this monstrous defensive end. "Nuke" was short for Nuclear Android because the man was totally obsessed with steroids.

Not that a lot of guys weren't. Steroids were about as common as Anacin in our locker room. I'd guess about half the guys on the team took them just to look good—to help them buff up—and another 20 to 25 percent took them *seriously* to get strong and put on weight. The percentage is even higher in the pros. I can always tell when a guy's doing serious steroids in the pros because he'll start the season at 270 pounds and *end* it at 280. You play twenty games in a season. You don't gain weight, you lose it. I know I lose about 10 pounds. And here these guys are having to cut their shorts because their legs don't fit in them anymore and it's *December*.

Most of the guys who took steroids in college were

offensive and defensive linemen. I'd go up to one guy especially, one of our starting linemen, with my shades on, sort of staggering up to him like the glare off of him was blinding me.

"Man, look at you!" I'd say. "You're radioactive! You're glowing! Turn the beams off, man! You're charging the whole place up!"

He'd always just mumble and go back to clean-and-jerking the chemistry building.

The smart guys never took steroids because we'd had too many biology courses. Steroids are just concentrated nuggets of testosterone, the male sex hormone. Some of us (ahem) had more than we needed of that. Line forms to the right, girls.

The scary thing about steroids is that they feel so good that they become really addictive, which is what happened to Nuke. It gives you this tremendous drive and intensity. You always want to go in and work out on the weights. It's a different kind of high, a total body high. You get to a point where you feel *soooo* good. You're strong as an ox. You're healthy. You're eating right. You're sleeping right.

But the problem is the side effects. Besides the dangers to your heart, it makes your muscles feel real tight. If you try to do any running, you feel like hell because your muscles are hurting so bad. The steroids are tightening your muscles so bad that they're not allowing the blood to pass through. That makes it painful.

A lot of the guys used steroids with some common sense, but a lot didn't, like Nuke. He was a maniac about 'roids. He had this friend who would get them for him on the black market. He'd experiment with all this new stuff, stuff that hadn't ever been tried.

He'd do pills and injections at the same time, sort of a John Belushi waiting to happen. He was strong as hell. He was only nineteen years old and he could bench press 530 pounds and squat 700.

But the problem was when he'd get out in the field, working his body, he'd be in real danger. He couldn't catch his breath and, of course, he couldn't move laterally at all. He looked like E.T. trying to rush the quarterback. One time he was out at practice and his face turned beet red and he just sort of lay down. The doctors checked his heart rate and it was three times faster than a normal human under the same circumstances.

Everybody tried to talk to him—me, other guys, the coaches, the doctors—but he just wouldn't listen. That's when we started taking bets on him. As it turned out, nobody has won yet because he was transferred to another school the next year. I still check the obits for him. I've got 1989 for ten bucks.

Steroids made you strong, but they made you about as quick as Raymond Burr. I pride myself on quickness *and* strength and that's why I never did the things. *Unless* I was injured and needed to get my injury rehabbed fast.

And that's exactly what happened to me after the national championship game against Penn State. I was banged up bad. I had a real bad shoulder. I couldn't raise it high enough to comb my hair. If you know me, that's an *emergency*. And I had a deep thigh bruise that hurt so bad I could hardly walk. The doctors told me it was going to take a long time to heal and that I might not be ready for spring practice. Well, the last time I wasn't ready for spring I played like hell the start of the next year and I couldn't afford that and neither could Oklahoma, I thought.

So I went to another doctor, who shall remain nameless, and he said if I didn't have time to rehab it, he could put me on Deca-Durabolin, a form of steroid, for six weeks, from February through March, and that would speed up the process. He said I'd be back to my bad-ass self in six weeks. So I did it and it healed up perfectly. By the middle of March I was in great shape again, so he took me off of them. That was that. Or so I thought.

What you've got to understand is that what I did through that doctor was perfectly legal, both by law and by the NCAA. It wasn't until later—in September, the start of the season—that the NCAA came out with a rule that said steroids were banned and they were going to randomly test players on bowl teams in December. Well, the steroids I took stay in your system for a year. That meant that I had broken a law before it ever *became* a law. It's sort of like a woman getting pregnant in March and then finding out in August that it's illegal to have babies.

But the amount of steroids I took was so small that when OU gave us a steroid test in September, just to prepare themselves for who might be in trouble when the NCAA came around, I passed. No problem.

Another drug test wasn't that big of a deal anyway. Football players are constantly being poked and prodded and made to piss into little jars. We had constant tests for pot and cocaine at OU. Guys would try to beat them all the time. They'd get a clean guy to piss in a Visine bottle for them and then tape it to the inside of a thigh before they went into the john for the test. But the trainer found out about that and from then on he'd stand there and watch you perform your duty. It was not only embarrassing, it was humiliating. "Seems like you're holding on to it longer than you need to, son."

Anyway, because I passed, I assumed the drug was out of my system after that. But between our last game against SMU and our Orange Bowl appearance against Arkansas, some weird things happened. I had to go to Los Angeles to do the Bob (No) Hope All-American show. One night I ordered some of those little hotel pizzas in my room. It turned out to be the mistake of my life. They made me sick as a dog. They ought to put a little Surgeon General's warning on the side of those pizzas: DO NOT EAT. TOXIC WASTE.

All the way home I was lying down on the plane. My stomach hurt so bad I was doubled over. The next night I had my girlfriend check me into the university hospital. I couldn't hold anything down. They said I had food poisoning. I had three IVs in me. I had lost fifteen pounds and there were only two weeks to go before we left for the Orange Bowl.

So guess who was kind enough to come visit me in the hospital the next day? You guessed it. The fine and friendly folks at your neighborhood NCAA.

The guy that came to see me in the hospital had little black eyes that were too close together and no chin. He looked like a high school equipment manager that wanted to stay in sports and the NCAA was the closest he could get. In his $99 Wal-Mart suit, he made a real fashion statement, which was: "Don't dress like me."

"We need a sample for the test," he said.

There I was, dehydrated like the Mohave desert, needing three IVs just to get fluid in me, and Junior Detective wants me to piss. I was so dry I hadn't pissed since I got in the place two days before.

"Uh, can you give me a day or two and I'll get back to you on that?" I said.

"You don't piss, you don't play," he said.

Very nice.

"How am I supposed to piss? I haven't pissed since I got in here."

"Start drinking as much water as you can."

Realizing I was stuck, I reached for the jug of water by the side of the bed.

"Wait!" he yelled, grabbing the water.

"What?" I said, jumping back.

"I'll get it myself. You might have put a diuretic in the water to screen the test."

That flipped me out.

"Right, right. That's exactly what I did. This whole thing is a charade. I checked myself into the hospital, let them stick three IVs in me, laid in this hospital bed, ate this horrible hospital food, just so that when you guys came to test me I could slip a diuretic in this bottle of water in order to screen your test. It's a helluva plan, ain't it? Just brilliant."

He got his own water anyway. Didn't matter. I couldn't piss. I tried and tried and nothing happened.

He looked at me like he was Dick Tracy and said, "Well, Mr. Bosworth. I guess you're ineligible."

If I could've worked up something out of my cotton mouth, I'd have spit on him.

I kept drinking water, hoping it would happen.

When I was finally ready, I called him and he came back.

It's no wonder, when you think about it, that I tested positive that day. The sample they got from me was from the dregs of my kidneys. They were scraping the bottom of them. Everybody else gave their sample with a healthy body. But that didn't matter to the NCAA. I flunked. I was out of the Orange Bowl. My name was going on the eleven o'clock news all over the country as a 'roidoid. That little shit walked out of the hospital like he'd just won the lottery.

When Oklahoma found out I'd flunked the NCAA test, they decided to test me themselves. I showed up negative for Deca-Durabolin. But I showed up positive for something called Dynabol, which I'd never taken in my life. Nice tests. What scares you is knowing that these tests can ruin people's *lives*. They give tests in the government for drugs and you can lose your job if you fail. And the tests aren't even reliable.

So we thought we had some legitimate bitches with the whole thing: (1) I wasn't healthy; (2) the tests weren't reliable; and (3) the drug was perfectly legal when I originally took it. How can you be convicted in December of something that wasn't a crime when you did it back in February? This is called NCAA logic.

We had more than enough to win in court. Lawyers told us that. All we were waiting on was the university to come around and back us up. You'd look stupid if your own school wasn't behind you. We didn't know how long that wait would be. Like forever.

The University of Oklahoma hung me out to dry. Left me alone on an island to fend for myself. Here I had taken a drug to speed my recovery so that I could help the team—the school—have another successful season, make a bundle in TV money and bowl money ($2 million per team in the Orange Bowl), and as soon as something went wrong with the method I used to recover, they cut the rope. The guy that had got the university more TV time and magazine covers and contribution money than their fund-raising committees could've gotten in twenty-five years was left twisting in the wind.

The funny thing is, Oklahoma started out saying they were behind us. We had legal counsel calling me every day, saying we'd get an injunction. If OU would've had any balls, they would have continued to back me up and we'd have won our case. Stanford went to bat for a swimmer the next year on the same principle and won. She refused to take the test on the grounds that it invaded her privacy. (Which it did. Do they make the debate team take drug tests? The star violinists? No.) And she won. But OU acted like I was some ex-brother-in-law they never wanted to see again.

And why was the NCAA in such a hurry to make a grand example out of me? One was because I had burned them before in print. They had stopped me from writing messages on my shoes and I ripped them. I had also ripped them on the ROTC poster thing. Two, that was their first year of the drug-testing program and they needed a big name to scare people straight right away. They got their big name all right. Stupid me.

The other stupid thing about it is that the NCAA's

rules didn't cover pot or coke. If I had been detected with either of those in my system, it would've been no problem. "Give 'em hell out there, son." But take a steroid as a doctor-prescribed treatment for an injury and it's "Adios, amigos." Welcome to Russia.

What is the point of the NCAA anyway? You could bust 70 percent of the guys in college for steroids if you wanted, but they don't. You could throw every major college in the slam for cheating, but they don't. You could get nearly every player for taking money, but they don't. The NCAA is thirty or so investigators in Kansas City trying to police a *big* business—college football—which means hundreds of colleges, thousands of players, tens of thousands of alumni, and uncountable sleazy agents. It's like being in a room surrounded by wild dogs and having only one bullet in your gun. You've got to shoot *somebody*. The problem is who they end up shooting is based on money and politics.

Anyway, that was only half of my problem. Getting kicked out of the Orange Bowl *wasn't* my fault. Doing something stupid in front of the nation and getting kicked off the team *was*. Okay, so I was having a bad month.

I flew down to the Orange Bowl after Christmas—Switzer took care of my ticket, but I still don't know how—and started plotting my little act of protest against the National Collegiate Assholes Association. And wouldn't the NCAA and the University of Oklahoma be thrilled to know who gave me the idea that caused all the trouble? Yessir, it was The King himself, Switzer.

He had given it to me at the Colorado game that

year. That's when we played Colorado and they told me that I couldn't write on my shoes. I had been writing various messages on them just for kicks. Like I'd write FRED on one and AKERS on the other, upside down, because that's how I figured he must write out his playbook. Then the refs came in the locker room and told me I couldn't write on my shoes anymore.

"Why not?" I asked one of them.

"No reason," the ref said. "The NCAA told us you couldn't."

"What does the NCAA care what I write on my shoes?"

"Don't know," he said. "But if you come out with anything written on your shoes, we're going to throw you out."

Typical NCAA. Slush funds everyplace, recruits getting picked up by a limousine with a prostitute inside, drug use going on like crazy, and they're worried about what I write on my shoes. They never did give a reason. Probably something like "If we let you write on your shoes, *everybody* will want to write on their shoes." Yeah, and before you know it, companies will be writing on shoes too, stuff like NIKE, ADIDAS, and CONVERSE.

So I had to paint my shoes black for that game. I was the only guy on the field wearing black shoes. Afterward, Switzer came up to me and said, "Look, do me a favor. Don't say anything about the shoes to the press after this."

I said, "That doesn't make sense. This whole thing doesn't make sense."

And he said, "I know. They're just a bunch of goddamn Communists up there."

And I said to myself, "He's right. They are just a bunch of Communists, taking away basic rights of people who happen to be athletes, rights they wouldn't even *think* of taking away from other people. They're the National Communists Against Athletes." Thanks, Barry. I stowed that line away.

In Miami my roommate, Grunt—Todd Granato— and I went all over Miami Beach, looking for a place to make up a T-shirt. We took an official Orange Bowl car to do it, which I thought was a nice touch. The T-shirt read: NCAA: NATIONAL COMMUNISTS AGAINST ATHLETES. Thanks, Switz.

I was allowed to stand on the sideline with the team for the game, so I brought it with me into the locker room and gave it to the manager to hold because I didn't want anybody asking me what it was. But somebody took it out and started showing it to people. When Switzer saw it, I guess he hated it, so he took it and hid it. That was The King's way of dealing with the problem. He didn't tell me not to use it, didn't yell at me about it, just hid it, hoping I wouldn't find it. Switzer never was any good at yelling at me.

When I found out, I got all pissed off. It was during the second quarter of the game and I told the manager to get his ass in the locker room at halftime and find it. I wasn't sure I was going to use it until I found out Switzer had stolen it. That made my mind up.

We went up 28–0 in the game in the third quarter. I could hear people changing channels all across the country. I decided it was then or never. The manager had found the shirt and I'd put it on underneath my jersey. So, right then, I whipped off the jersey. I'll bet I didn't have it off for more than thirty seconds when—*phoom*—the cameras were on me. I had it off maybe for a minute, total. But by then the damage was done.

I knew as soon as I saw the cameras turn to me that I'd made a mistake, that I'd gone too far. I always go pretty damn far (but never too far) over the line of good judgment, over the line of just being stupid. All I was trying to do was make something fun out of a screwed-up situation. I thought people would laugh. But once I had it off, I realized it looked like I was really serious. If I had one minute to take back in my life, it'd be that one.

I know I was wrong, but there was one thing that pissed me off about the T-shirt incident. The night before it happened, Don Criqui, the play-by-play guy calling the game for NBC, came up to me at a party and told me, "I just think it's wonderful that you're taking this stand against the NCAA in the papers. You're 100 percent right." But when I unveiled the T-shirt on TV, Criqui ripped me unmercifully. Nothing I hate more than two faces on one person. That showed me no class.

Still, I thought I'd take some grief like that—in the press—and that would be the end of it. After all, Switzer never said a thing to me on the plane home. But when we got back, he must've gotten a call from somebody because all of a sudden there was tremendous pressure on him to get rid of me. From what I'd heard, someone told him he was taking a lot of grief from some of the old prune-skinned donors. So somebody must have knuckled under. Instead of telling them, "Look, he's a student. Students make mistakes. They learn from them,'' they wanted Switzer to kick me off the team.

Switzer called me in his office, sat me down, and never looked me in the eye the whole time.

"Brian," he said. "I'm getting all kinds of pressure from everybody. Everybody's pissed off about this T-shirt thing. If it was up to me, I wouldn't make this decision, but it's not up to me. I'd rather you didn't come back for next year's season."

That hurt, hearing it. I mean, I love the state of Oklahoma and I love the school. I didn't want people hating me there. My grandmother lives there, for Chrissakes. But Switzer and I knew it was sort of a charade in the first place. He knew I wasn't planning on coming back for my last season. I knew it. This way Switzer could appease Horton—look big to Horton—without really losing a thing. And besides, I felt bad about it, bad enough to let Switzer off the hook.

"I'm sorry this happened," I said. "I'm sorry if this puts any pressure on you or causes you any trouble at all. I apologize." I was feeling really lousy about the whole thing.

But when I got home, Gary Wichard, who later became my agent, was on the phone.

"You're screwed," he said.

"Why?"

"Because you just lost all our leverage against the NFL."

He was right. I'd totally forgotten. I was all set to graduate early, but without the threat that I could come back for my last year of college and *not* go where an NFL team drafted us, I was up the creek. If I went through the supplemental draft and Indianapolis or some other godforsaken place took me, I'd *have* to go there. I had no other options. My whole plan, what I'd dreamed about since I was a freshman, was about to bite it.

I called Switzer the next day.

"Coach, it's Brian. Look, I've got a problem. I was hurt at first about this thing, but now I'm pissed. You just took some serious money out of my mouth for no reason at all." I explained my problem with the NFL.

I said, "You knew I wasn't coming back and I knew I wasn't coming back. I want to do something that's going to make some sense. Otherwise, I'll go down to the paper and rip the hell out of Oklahoma. I'll go through it all. I'll tell how you didn't go to bat for me in this whole thing. I come in contact with recruits all the time and you know recruits listen to what I say. It wouldn't be in your best interest to screw me!"

What also had pissed me off is that when Switzer told the papers what had happened between us, he made it sound like big strong King was booting spoiled-ass Boz off the team. He didn't mention anything about the mutual agreement we had come to. I didn't appreciate that either, so I told him. I'd set the papers straight on exactly what happened.

So what did Switzer do? He took it like a man. He stepped right up and helped me out. He didn't really have a choice, but he didn't have to do everything he did. He said, "Okay, this is what we'll do . . ."

His plan was sharp. I would write a letter to him and to the people of Oklahoma, begging their forgiveness, saying I was wrong and didn't want to go out this way, saying I wanted a chance to play one more year for their great university. He would receive the letter and show it to the papers and say that he was "very impressed." Then he'd say that he was so impressed at my heartfelt apology that he might consider reinstating me to the team "at a later date." I'd have my leverage back and he could tell Horton that he wasn't *really* going to let me back, only that he felt sorry for me.

And that's exactly what happened. Pat Hanlon and I typed up this beautiful letter, in which I apologized for everything wrong in the world, up to and including dishwasher spots. I didn't mean a word of it, but I was *scared*. This was millions of NFL dollars we were talking about. This could make the difference in living in a place I wanted to live or in some hole. I was just hoping people knew me well enough to know that I would never take back opinions that I think are the truth.

As it turned out, it worked perfectly, and Switzer is the one to thank. I wouldn't have the team I have now—or the money—if not for him. I respect him for that.

My relationship with Switzer was strange that way. I respected him for a lot of things. I hated him for a lot of things. I think I'll start another chapter.

CHAPTER
12

The King and I

Let me tell you a quick story about Barry Switzer and yours truly.

This was just after we'd lost to Washington in the Orange Bowl my freshman year. I was one of the guys helping the coaches recruit. Guys would come in for official trips and I'd be one of the guys that helped out. I'd show up at a party and talk to them a little bit.

They'd put these recruits in some cottages they had on campus for people who visited. They were really nice. The walls were all solid-oak paneling and there were TVs and kitchens and everything.

Naturally, we had to have some malted beverages to cool our throats during all this talking, so one night at one of these cottages, somebody brought over a keg. Somewhere in there, probably near the bottom of the keg, the talking stopped and the search-and-destroying began. We got so drunk that we started taking the place apart. We took the electric socket plates out and threw them through windows, like Frisbees. We found some steak knives and took target practice on the oak walls. That pretty much ruined the paneling, so we ripped it out to save workmen the trouble later. We took all the pictures off the wall and put our fists through them. We turned the TV upside down and watched it standing on our heads. This was all part of the recruiting process. Got to give the youngsters an idea of the kind of life they can expect at OU. The only thing we didn't have was Buster Rhymes and his Uzi, but we couldn't be expected to think of *everything*. We must've done two or three thousand dollars' worth of damage to that cottage. The next day Switzer called a team meeting about it. He was pissed. He wanted to know who did it.

I raised my hand first. Then a couple of other guys who were there raised their hands. We were fessing up.

But guess what? Switzer never even yelled at me. Didn't even acknowledge that my hand was up. He reamed the other guys new holes, but he never said a thing to me, the man who had his hand up first.

That's the best example of how things were between The King and I. Somehow nothing I could do was enough to get Switzer pissed off at me. And the thing was, I think I secretly *wanted* him to be pissed at me. I wanted him to discipline me. I wanted to know that he cared for what happened to me, that I wasn't just a big piece of meat who could run a 4.59 forty for him. I see the same things happening now with Jamelle Holieway. He can do no wrong for Switzer and Switzer does *everything* for him. Lets him drive his car, lets him use his car phone, lets him come late to practice, lets him have run of the land.

After a while you do things just to see what would make him bust. I'd go late to meetings. Not just a few. Every meeting. Ten, twenty minutes late. Nothing happened. Switzer's Rule was always in effect, no matter what the circumstance. If you were a great player who helped *him* look good, who helped him keep his job, you could do anything, and he let me do *anything*. Even though, deep down, I knew it wasn't the best for me. Maybe if I had just told him I wanted his help, our relationship—my career— would have been different.

But as it was, Switzer never helped me grow up. I had to do it all on my own and it took me, I'll admit, a long time. The King could've sat me down a thousand times and said, "Look, I'll let you do what you want, but let me give you a few tips on dealing with people." Or . . . "Hey, why don't you try this with the next interview? Give another side to yourself." He never told me I was getting used by the press. Never told me how important your national image is. He never took me aside and said, "Watch out for this or that."

Switzer once said: "Brian Bosworth is a great player. I like Bosworth. Brian Bosworth is a super football player. I'd like to coach a bunch of them. I just didn't like The Boz, the media egomaniac." The funny thing about that statement is that anybody that knows The King knows that the man is on the All-Time All-Ego Five. He's every bit my ego equal. If anything, he laid the foundation for my ego because he never tried to shape it at all.

I think I know what that is. When he looked at me, Switzer saw someone he had always wanted to be. My lifestyle appealed to him—the partier, the guy who does what he wants, says what he wants. In himself, he saw a guy who had to suck up to all sorts of people—especially the new university president, Frank (my future Postmaster) Horton. He didn't like what he had become. He liked what I was. My theory about Switzer is true. I know it because he told me one night.

We were both out on the town. I was half-drunk. Switzer was blotto. We ran into each other at an Italian restaurant.

"Bozzzzzz!" he yelled at me across the room.

"Coach," I said.

It wasn't unusual for us to see each other out on the town. The King loved to party and so did I. We're a lot alike in a lot of ways. We like to have a good time. The King is divorced and not because his wife didn't like his cooking. Until I got there, The King was the ruler of Norman, Oklahoma, and he could have as much fun as he wanted—any way he wanted.

"Bozzzzz!" he said again. "You sumbitch."

He seemed happy. "Why are you calling me a sumbitch, Coach?" I was willing to bite.

"Because, *Bozzzzz*. I wish I could say all those things you say and get away with it, but, dang, they'd just nail me to the dang wall!"

"Coach, you taught me you could do anything you want as long as you do one thing and that's win. And no one can bitch about you because you win."

"Well, it doesn't work exactly like that. I'm not in your position. I've got to be a little more tactful with my job. Dang."

Switz and I *are* a lot alike. He's brash and outspoken. So am I. He likes to step on toes for fun. So do I. He's colorful and a partier. So am I. He was an honor student at Arkansas and a damn good college football player who loved the game. So was I. We both know our way around people. We've been to a hundred of the same cocktail parties and we can both adapt and fit in—whether its rednecks in NUKE PHIL DONAHUE hats or history professors in bow ties. We're both overachievers, guys who want to win at all costs and will walk over anybody to do it.

But that was the problem. It's like those old Westerns. Norman, Oklahoma, just warn't big enough for the two of us, pilgrim. And the bigger I got, the more jealous he got, and the more dangerous our relationship got.

But I don't think that was my fault. He knew what I was after at Oklahoma. From the very first day he wrapped his full-length fur coat around me in the school cafeteria back at MacArthur High, he knew. And I told him again the day I decided to go to Oklahoma. I remember it like it was yesterday.

I asked him if he and I could go alone into his office and I said, "Coach, why are you recruiting me?"

That pissed him off. "Son," he said with his chest all pumped up, "are you *serious* about asking me that question?"

"Yeah."

"I want you to play. I know what you can do."

"Coach, I want to win. But I want people to know I can play too. I want recognition. I want to be an All-American."

I was already thinking about the NFL at that point. I had my scheme all set. While the rest of my high school buddies were thinking about whether they were going to get the top bunk or the bottom bunk in college, I was already planning through the day I retired. I made up my mind to graduate early and have the NFL over a barrel. It was a complex with me. After playing my ass off for a high school coach that didn't know his elbow from an end around, I'd gotten sort of a complex about being given credit for what I was doing. I *knew* I was a good player. Now I had to convince everybody else. And I needed Switzer to let me show them.

"I know that you didn't get one iota of recognition out of high school," Switzer said. "I've seen film on you, son. And I believe you're a winner. If you come here and do the things that I think you can do, why I'll give you all the publicity you want. The University of Oklahoma is a stage that will allow you to draw as many curtain calls as you want. If you deserve it, I'll make you the biggest player that's ever been through here."

I wonder if he'd like to have those words back now.

What you have to understand to start with is that Barry Switzer is an insecure person. We all are. But Switzer is more insecure than almost anybody I know. He had a rough childhood. His father was a bootlegger in Arkansas. His mother committed suicide. So it seems like he's been living his whole life trying to prove to people that he belongs, trying to show people that he's made it, that he's not just some bootlegger's son. And he has done that. He'll go down as one of the greatest college football coaches in history. Only Knute Rockne and Frank Leahy, both of Notre Dame, have a higher career winning percentage than Switzer. Nobody's won more national championships and no active coach has won more games.

But sometimes he tries too hard to show people that the bootlegger's son has made it big. For a man who was fifty-one in 1988, his life isn't exactly a bedrock. He's not married. He's got a girlfriend that he has an off-and-on relationship with. He hits the town a lot, staying out late. He's been in all kinds of business trouble all his life. He's kind of like Gary Hart. His judgment is not always the best.

He's so insecure that only when he owns the whole kingdom, the whole town, does he feel safe. And that's where he and I started to have problems. I took over his town and he couldn't handle it. Not that I was trying to take it over. The people were just handing it to me.

It started out with press conferences. I'd have so many interview requests the week before a game my sophomore and junior seasons that we had to start scheduling press conferences for me. I'd hold mine the same day Switzer would hold his. Only there'd be fifty guys at mine and fifteen at his. And all the guys at his would want to ask him about was me. That really pissed him off.

He had no idea what I was up to next and that pissed him off too. I'd needle him about it. One time I was filming some charity commercial and all of a sudden Switzer walked in.

"What's going on here?" he said, perturbed.

"Oh, just another commercial, Coach," I said.

"What is it?"

"Miller Lite," I said.

He shook his head and closed the door. I don't think he wanted to know if I was kidding or not.

But I knew my status was starting to bug him because pretty soon I'd start reading quotes from him like "*I'm* the one who makes the decisions around here, not The Boz." He'd get madder and madder at me, even though I wasn't doing a thing on purpose. I wasn't trying to step on his territory. It was always Switzer's team and I knew it. It was jealousy, pure and simple, and it was real easy to see.

He obviously had never had to deal with somebody like me before. He'd always brought in good players who he'd take to a certain height and that would be it. "Fine, appreciate it. See you later." They could get pretty high, but not up to his throne. All they could get to was his boot level. But he didn't count on somebody who would take advantage of the situation. He didn't count on someone who would come in and make his name as big as he possibly could, someone who knew how to use the media and wasn't afraid to use it. He never figured that more people would come to an Oklahoma game to see the player than the coach, but it happened. I outdrew him in mail probably five-to-one. And pretty soon people started saying, "Who runs Oklahoma football? Barry or Boz?"

So when the steroid thing happened, followed by the T-shirt, and Horton called his office that day, you can see where Switzer's mind was. Here I was, a threat to his throne, and here was Horton on the other end with a way to get rid of me. Not only that, but Switzer was afraid of Horton. That was Horton's first year on the job after replacing William Banowski. Switzer wasn't afraid of Banowski because Banowski knew what the hell he was doing. Banowski would let Switzer run the football program like he'd always run it. It was one of the most successful in the country, so why not? But when Banowski left, Horton came in and wanted to get his paws into everything.

The guys on the team always thought of Horton as a wanna-be. He wanted to be a player or he wanted to be a coach or he wanted to be a ball boy or something because he was constantly hanging around our locker room, before and after the games, and on the sideline during it. To me, that sucked. Nobody on the team wanted him there, so why was he there? We knew why. He was new on the job and wanted to show that he belonged. And there's no better way to show the state of Oklahoma that you belong than to be taken in by the OU football team.

Personally, hanging around a bunch of sweaty guys in jocks doesn't show me squat. Why didn't he just stick to his office and try to impress people with the job he was doing? I hated him horning in on us. I mean, I never walked into *his* office while he was trying to work and stuck my two cents' in. "C'mon, Frankie! The guy is ready to spring big! Get another five grand out of the son of a bitch!"

Horton didn't know what the hell to make out of me. He was terrified of me. Here I was, far and away the most well-known person in Oklahoma—and the most well-known Oklahoman in the country—and I was a loose cannon that went off wherever and whenever I pleased. To a P.R.-paranoiac like Horton, I was Ozzy Osbourne with a headless bat in my hand.

Horton was so nervous about me that he would open my mail, read it, and answer it, signing his name instead of mine. He was so worried that I might be doing some harm to the university's image, that I might be hurting the university's ability to raise money, that he was violating the hell out of my civil rights along the way. But what Frankie didn't understand is that for every letter I got from some mother who was upset about something I said, I'd get ten letters from kids who were behind me all the way and said they'd like to go to Oklahoma because of me. I handled my mail just fine by myself. When I'd get a letter from some idiot, saying, "Why don't you go live in Russia, you Nazi slime pig!" I'd always send them an autographed picture with something like "I'm glad I have finally driven you to this lunacy. Now you can seek help. Warmly, Brian Bosworth, No. 44." Now, I had some worm answering my letters with something like . . .

Dear Mrs. Fitchelman (or whatever):

The University of Oklahoma, a fine and upstanding institution, deeply regrets any hurt feelings Mr. Brian Bosworth may have caused you and your family by his recent actions.

Please know that Mr. Bosworth has been duly disciplined. In no way do his remarks represent the University of Oklahoma.

Sincerely,
President Frank E. Horton, R.I.P.

Maybe Frank was sick the day they explained the Constitution in grade school.

I found out about Horton's tricks through a friend of mine on the team who was close with someone in Horton's office. I'll leave their name out of it because God knows they have gone through enough hell having to work for Horton in the first place. It bothered them that Horton was: one, opening my mail; and two, answering it for me.

They finally got so worried about it that they called my buddy.

"Does Brian know he's doing this?"

"I don't think so," my buddy said.

So the person in Horton's office Xeroxed a bunch of Horton's replies and gave them to my buddy. I've got all the Xeroxes at home in case anybody wants to see them. I was handed the letters at the team breakfast just before the Colorado game and I flipped out.

Just then Horton came into the banquet room. What nice timing. I practically tore his puny head off his measly neck.

"What the f__ are these?" I said, waving the letters in his face.

"Well, those are just letters that I didn't want to bug you with," he said.

"Bug me with?"

"Yeah, I figured that it would be a good opportunity to answer them and maybe help you out a little bit."

Right. Sort of the way Iran "helps out" Iraq.

"Look, man. You aren't helping me out. All you're trying to do is save a few donations. All you're doing is violating my privacy. I could sue you right here and now and you know it. Don't do anything to *help me out* anymore, got it? I'm capable of opening and answering my own mail."

"You have no right to talk to me that way."

"Look, you open another letter of mine and I'm calling the police."

Not only did he never open another letter of mine, I don't think he finished his eggs that day.

I had caught him red-handed doing something not only illegal but morally wrong and embarrassed him in front of the whole team and all the coaches. After that I knew he was looking for a way to try and get rid of my ass. And when I wore that T-shirt on national TV, it was like handing Mr. Tight Ass a gift-wrapped excuse to blow me out of the water. Happy birthday.

So Horton called Switzer and Switzer had to decide what he wanted to do with me. I don't care how much pressure he got, there was no way Frank Horton, first year cub president, was going to fire The King. No way. Switzer had to make a choice. And at that moment—forget what happened afterward—he decided to sell me down the river. He kicked me off the team.

Sometimes I think he did it because he imagined I was a lot of trouble. What he didn't understand is that I could and did deal with all of them myself. Hell, Switzer couldn't handle his *own* problems. No wonder he was surprised I could handle mine. If he had a fight with his girlfriend or a problem with a lawyer or a bank, he'd mope around the office all day. He could never leave his home troubles at home. He took everything to work.

And I guess he took my troubles on his shoulders too. I had my own plan, my own style, and it puzzled him. He thought he had my burdens too, but he didn't. I could never get it through his head that I could handle my own affairs, that they weren't his responsibility. Like after I said UCLA was a semi-doormat, he called me in his office and started lecturing me. But before he got very far, I said one thing.

"Coach, just a minute. Were they worth a shit or not?"

"No . . ."

"Well, then it's not your problem. I'll handle it. I'll take the heat."

I don't think he could understand that. In all the times he got in trouble at Oklahoma, I never saw him come forward and say, "Look, I'm going to write an apology letter to the university." He would never do that. But he made *me* do it. Twice.

What he forgot that day—the day he fried me— was the fact that our class had saved his job, and I was the leader of that class. He'd had three four-loss seasons in a row and people in Oklahoma were starting to bubble the tar. They'd almost had him fired the last two seasons running. Switzer was turning Oklahoma into Oklahoma State. He got lazy with all his success. He stopped recruiting all the great athletes. He thought he could win off the name of Oklahoma alone. People started catching up with him. He had two or three bad recruiting years and that killed him. He had forgotten his number one rule: players win games, not coaches.

That was never more true than in Switzer's case. Switzer isn't a coach. He's a P.R. man, hand shaker, TV show host, and the best recruiter in the country. But he doesn't coach jack anymore. Coach Donnan is in charge of the offense and Coach Gibbs runs the defense. Switzer comes late to practice—if at all— and leaves early. He goes home or up to his office and makes calls. All I know is I can't remember him ever staying through an entire practice. And he and I never shared Word One about playing defense at Oklahoma. For one, he never talks to the defense. Two, he wouldn't know what to say to somebody on defense if it was going to save his life. I guess he used to know the wishbone inside and out, but he doesn't even know that anymore.

But who cares? He hires great people. His job is to get the great players. And he had stopped doing that until my class came in. The year I started playing, we got the Big Eight title back for him and never gave it back. It wasn't Switzer blocking and tackling out there. All the time I was there I never saw Switzer strap on a jock. It was the players. And not only did the players win for him, most of our class graduated on time. People were always on his back about his players not graduating, but we gave him a break. Especially me. I graduated a year ahead of schedule.

But when the pressure was on to get rid of me he forgot all that. He caved in to his own insecurity. At that moment he was just another politician. Just another two-dimensional cardboard face in a sport coat with no depth to him.

That was the way our relationship ended, really. Anything after that was pointless because I knew he had burned me when it counted. And that was too bad because there were a lot of things I liked about Switzer and it's funny, but the more I'm away from him, the more I remember the good things than the bad.

For one thing, Switzer always let me look and dress the way I wanted. He'd always stick up for me on my hair. "What the hell does that have to do with winning and losing?" he'd say when people would ask about it. "What does that have to do with telling you what kind of a competitor he is? I'd rather coach guys who express themselves than a bunch of clones.'' I respected that. He was open-minded to look *under* my hair to see what was in my brain.

He never pulled an Ayatollah Paterno on us either. He never put up a list on the team bulletin board: WHAT YOU CAN SAY AND WHAT YOU CAN'T SAY—AND ANYBODY THAT SCREWS UP GETS A FINGER CHOPPED OFF. Switzer was never sure what *he* was going to say, much less try to tell us what we could say.

I remember after the Penn State win, Switzer was talking to us and I remember being as happy for him as I was for us. It's on the OU highlight film from that year—me looking up at him—and every time I see it, I get the chills. It reminds me of what he did for me. He never tried to muzzle me or put a harness on me and he's the only one. When I went to the pros, Seattle coach Chuck Knox *talked about* not muzzling me, but then he went right ahead and tried to muzzle me just the same. But Switzer never did.

He was a players' coach that way. Whenever we'd lose, he wouldn't scream at anybody. He never made a big speech. He'd be cool about it. He'd say it was his fault. He'd take full responsibility. He'd try to make us feel a lot better about ourselves. But we knew it wasn't his fault when we lost any more than it was to his credit when we won. He got us there and let his staff coach us. That was fine by me.

Maybe he's forgotten some of the bad things about me too. The last time I went back to Norman he was very friendly to me.

''I really like the way you've been handling everything this year,'' he said to me. ''You're learning a lot and you're doing the right thing.''

You don't think he found out I was writing a book, do you? Naaaaaaah.

CHAPTER
13

55 Minus
44 Equals
11 Million

My arrival in Seattle to begin life in the NFL was about like any other rookie's first day. There were only about two hundred people at the Sea-Tac airport waiting for me to get off the plane; only about ten television cameras stuck, literally, in my ear, trying to get up-close-and-personal shots of my earrings. Those camera crews had staked out every flight from Dallas and Oklahoma City those last two days, hoping to catch my historic first steps on Seattle soil. What am I, the Pope?

I didn't know it yet, but the people of Seattle were going way overboard already. The radio stations were playing a song about me, sung to the tune of ''La Bamba,'' with ''Bosworth'' replacing ''Bamba.'' And they had gifts waiting too. They gave me a certificate for a free personalized driveway (complete with my name and uniform number embossed in stone), a pair of $350 Italian shoes, and a hundred condoms from the Seattle AIDS Society. The driveway I'll never use. For someone who is trying to keep people from knocking on his door all night, what's he going to do with a personalized driveway. What's *anybody* going to do with a personalized driveway? The shoes were red, so I don't wear them. And the condoms weren't even lubricated, so I gave them to a pretty good hound on the team. Knowing the guy, they were probably gone in about two weeks. Anyway, I appreciated the gifts. It's the thought that counts, right?

I didn't know about all that then, but as our plane pulled up to the gate and I saw all those people with their noses pressed to the window, I knew that if I thought my life would be more peaceful and orderly in the pros, I must've been demented. This was far worse than anything in Norman. This was far worse than anything I'd seen anywhere. It looked like *The Day of the Locusts* out there.

But, not to be humble or anything, who can blame them? They wanted to see the man that had held up the NFL, the man that had turned the NFL draft on its ear and turned it into a Supermarket Sweepstakes, the guy who had just signed an $11 million, ten-year, no-cut, all-guaranteed contract to play for the Seattle Seahawks. Excuse me while I read that sentence again.

That moment in the Sea-Tac airport was really the end of the grand scheme I'd had since I was a freshman in college. Like I said, I knew from the start that I would graduate early and play by my own rules, not the NFL's, so I could go wherever I wanted. I didn't want to play for a loser. I can't stand losing. I had too much losing when I played in high school to ever want to lose that way again. That's why I chose Oklahoma and that's why I set up this scheme. I wasn't going to play for Green goddamn Bay. Too close to Ray Nitschke.

To do all this, I knew I needed an agent. But I wasn't going to be brain-dead and sign early like a lot of guys. That's a real NCAA no-no. A lot of college players signed early with agents, took cars from them, sometimes drugs, got all their bills paid for and everything. Not bright. I took out a loan against my future earnings potential my junior year and lived off that. The loan wasn't payable until my rookie year in the pros.

Still, I knew who I was going to sign with the minute I graduated: Gary Wichard, an agent out of New York. Gary had played some small-college quarterback at C.W. Post, and he was cool. Plus, I trusted him, unlike so many other sleazebags I had to chase away from my door in four years at OU. You get hit on constantly by agents in college, or by friends of agents. Even pro players call and try to sign you with their guy. Howie Long of the Raiders called me to see if I wanted to hook up with his guy. I didn't even *know* Howie Long, much less his guy.

Gary was my guy and our plan was simple. We'd graduate early and then have the leverage against whoever took us in the supplemental draft. The supplemental draft is a special draft the NFL sets up for guys who graduate early—only a few have even tried it so far. The way it works is they take the drafting order for the regular draft—worst team goes first— and give them lottery tickets. If you're the worst team, you get twenty-eight tickets. If you're the best, you get one. Then they put them in a barrel and spin it and draw one out. I suggested Vanna White do the spinning. The team would get me and I'd get Vanna. "Yes, Vanna, I'll take a T and an A."

Anyway, if I didn't like the team that won the lottery, they'd be forced to trade me, knowing that I could always go back to Oklahoma and go through the draft again after my senior season. Anybody that took me better be damn sure I wanted to go there or they could lose a number one choice. And that's very bad P.R.

So we sent out "Dear John" letters to the teams we didn't want to play for: everybody but the two New York teams, the two L.A. teams, Chicago, and Philadelphia. That, of course, didn't mean anything because the team I really wanted to play for was Tampa Bay. We set up the New York-L.A. smoke-screen to give Tampa Bay owner Hugh Culverhouse more room to work a deal. We didn't want the other owners trying to keep me away from him.

Tampa Bay seemed perfect to me. They had only a thirty-five-thousand season tickets base, so they needed a draw. We figured they'd be desperate. I talked to Culverhouse right after the Orange Bowl and he told me he wanted Vinny Testaverde and me. I loved the idea of playing there. It was Florida, so the weather was nice, the conference is weak—except for Chicago—so it wouldn't take long to be a winner. And Culverhouse owns 70 percent of all the undeveloped land in Sarasota, Florida. He was willing to discuss putting some land in my contract. That land was worth about $400,000 a lot. I wanted about five lots. That stuff would've skyrocketed. He said he'd find a way to work a trade for me if they didn't win the lottery. I really thought he would.

There were other teams we would've signed with, too, that we didn't mention to the press. I would've played in Denver. I love the mountains, love to ski, and, after watching them play their last two Super Bowls, God knows they need some defense. I was willing to go to Miami or Washington or San Diego or San Francisco or Seattle too. Anyplace that was livable and was a winner—or could be a winner soon without half the teams in the NFL dying in a plane crash. I just didn't want to play for St. Louis or Indianapolis or Detroit or places like that.

I was ready to take loads of shit from those cities. I knew they'd all take it like I was napalming their town. I wasn't trying to make them feel lousy about their city. I'm sure people in Buffalo think it's the next best thing to Paris, but I just don't happen to agree. I just wanted people in Buffalo to know that I play my best when I'm happiest. In Buffalo I wouldn't have been happy. So if *I* was Buffalo, I wouldn't take me.

It's interesting that in all the truckloads of rip jobs people did on me around the country, nobody once mentioned that Mr. Glee Club, John Elway of the Broncos, did pretty much the same thing coming out of college. He was drafted by Baltimore and refused to go. At least I informed everyone that I had no interest in going. But nobody ever brought that up. I suppose it's because Elway has the look that reminds them of some surfer boy on *Gidget*. Personally, with those teeth of his, he reminds me of Mr. Ed.

What I wasn't ready for is the people who didn't think I had a *right* to get around the draft in the first place. I graduated from OU's business school in four years just so I could do all this and, amazingly enough, some people didn't even think I had the right to do *that*.

Yet if you went up to any big-business, ultra-right-wing John Birch Society CEO in the country and asked him, ''Do you think every American should have the freedom to choose where he wants to work and live and with which company?"

"Damn right," he'd say. "That's a basic American freedom. That's what this country was founded on."

"Good, then you have no objection to what Brian Bosworth is doing?"

"What's he doing?"

"Writing letters to all the NFL teams, telling them whether he will play there or not."

"No! What right does he have to do that? The NFL draft has been working just fine for years. He's a spoiled . . ."

"But I thought you said choosing where you want to work is a basic American freedom."

"Well, ahem, uh . . ."

"That's what this country was founded on."

"Sure, but mmmmm, uh . . ."

People are two-faced when it comes right down to it and that's too bad. A lot of those people are ugly enough as it is.

A lot of people, though, loved it. I mean, it *was* different, taking the big bad NFL and dragging it around by its nose. I know I loved it. This was just the kind of big change I liked to make. Sticking it to the fat cats, changing rules that make no sense. And the NFL is chock-full of bullshit rules that are anti-American. What gives the NFL the right to keep someone who *hasn't* graduated yet from earning his living in the NFL? Why does every other sport allow athletes to become free agents, to choose where they want to work and live, but not the NFL? Why does every other sport have a human being for a commissioner while the NFL has a guy with a face like a turtle without a shell?

On the day of the lottery we staked ourselves out in a New York hotel and waited for the news. Vanna did not draw. The winner was . . . Seattle.

Seattle?

I'd heard Seattle was beautiful and I didn't want to go there and fall in love with the place and screw up my plan. So we decided we'd stay away. Meantime, we checked it out and noticed that the Seahawks were scheduled to play seven nationally televised games that year, as many as the Giants. Our grand scheme was national endorsements and movies after that, so the more exposure the better. And even better than that was knowing that they were being picked up to go to the Super Bowl. Nobody wants a Super Bowl ring more than me. Not that I'd wear it, of course. Maybe I'd use it as a doorstop.

Still, I wasn't changing my plan. I still wanted to play for Tampa. I told the press conference that day, "They've gotten the letter. They know the deal." But it wasn't long before the phone was ringing in our hotel room. It was Chuck Knox, the Seahawks' head coach, the same guy who'd gotten my agent, Gary, into the Senior Bowl in 1971. Small world.

"We're not going to negotiate, Chuck," Gary said.

"At least do us the common courtesy of meeting [Seattle's general manager] McCormack and me face-to-face," Knox said. "Do it for me."

"All right. I'll do it for you," said Gary. "But we're not going to negotiate."

So what'd we do? We negotiated.

One thing I found out about the Seahawks is that

they do everything—well, almost everything—first-class. For this meeting, they rented an entire restaurant in Las Colinas, Texas, which is in Irving. They didn't want anybody bugging us. Chuck and I sat in another room and talked about fishing while McCormack and Gary talked money. The only thing Chuck said to me was "I won't muzzle you. I'll let you be yourself." I liked that.

It took a lot of wrangling, but eventually they threw a deal at us that just knocked us on our butts. We thought they'd give us the standard B.S. offer—$600,000 a year or so. But they were *serious*. They had to be serious to get this far into it. There wouldn't have been much pressure from their fans if they'd just backed off. But they went full-speed ahead anyhow. Still, what they offered us just wasn't *quite good enough*. We told them to trade us. And we walked out of the restaurant.

But after a while I started getting a little nervous. Seattle wasn't making any more offers and they weren't talking trade with anybody, even though we were being told Tampa Bay and Philadelphia were chomping at the bit to get me. I would've loved to play for Buddy Ryan. How's a guy as loud as him going to even *hear* my act?

Things were going bad. Gary and I were starting to talk about what I was going to do that year. No way I was going back to Graduate School in Norman. Going back was just a charade for the newspapers in the first place. I got so worried I started considering stupid things. Like some promoter offered me $50,000 just to stand in the corner with Hulk Hogan during Wrestlemania 12 or whatever it was. We turned it down, but it would've been fun.

The wrestling people love me. I've had offers of more than $1 million a year to wrestle professionally. Of course, if I did become a pro wrestler, I'd have to tone my act down a little.

Danny Sheridan, that Las Vegas oddsmaker guy, even set some odds against teams signing me, sort of The Boz Derby. The odds against Seattle signing me were 1–3; against them trading me, 1–1; my sitting out season, 5–1; Philadelphia signing me, 1–1; Tampa, 8–5; Rams, 2–1; Jets, 3–1; Giants, 5–1; Raiders, 10–1; odds against me going out of my mind, 5–2.

What we did do is scare Seattle with a movie career. I've had *beaucoups* offers from studios—what, with this face?—but we decided to do a quick little thing with HBO on one of their "First and Ten" episodes. I did it in East Los Angeles in about half a day. O. J. Simpson was in it. I didn't even read the script. I walked in and they got me in a uniform and started filming. I played a character named . . . surprise . . . Brian Bosworth. Only I was a halfback. Makes me sick to think of it: me on offense. This was a real slam-bam job. The writer was still writing my lines while they were shooting the scene. He'd say, "Quick, read this," while the camera was rolling. I held almost no hope of me getting an Emmy out of it. But it served its purpose. Seattle now knew we could spend the year in Hollywood and not starve.

I don't know if that did it or what, but not long afterward, McCormack was on the phone.

"Look, you draw up a proposal that you think is fair," he said.

Thank you very much. We did: $9 million and

something over seven years. Then McCormack drew up something different. Eventually we got it drawn to $11 million over ten years. It included a $2.5 million loan for ten years. The salary started at $300,000 the first year and went up $100,000 a year until 1992. Then it went to $1 million a year and up $100,000 every year after that. Best of all, it was guaranteed against injury for the full ten years. Go, Seahawks.

I have a feeling we scared them with the HBO thing, though, because Seattle wrote into the contract that if I left the team to start a movie career, I'd have to give back the signing bonus. So breathe easy, William Hurt. You'll still get the good roles for a while.

It's funny, though. Once I signed, people thought I had the $11 million under my pillow or in my passbook account. I made $300,000 my rookie year. That's good, but it ain't the moon. I was twenty-three. Mike Tyson made $60 million when he was twenty-one. Still, people were pissed. They kept saying, ''Eleven million? The whole Seattle franchise only cost sixteen million!'' Hey, don't try to make me feel guilty. I went to college. I studied marketing. Whatever the market will bear, right? What pissed me off is that my salary went public so quickly. I don't think it's anybody's business how much money people make. I don't go around asking presidents of corporations, ''Excuse me, sir. How much money are you making? Really? Is that all? Joe Cashola over at IBM is making a helluva lot more than you are. How do you feel about that? Doesn't that just byte your chips?''

Freddie Young, Seattle's starting strong-side linebacker, got a little hacked when he heard what I signed for, probably because he'd signed the day before for $250,000. I didn't mind that he was unhappy. What I did mind was that he went to the papers with it. I thought that was shitty. Shoulda tried HBO, Freddie.

That's about when I arrived at Sea-Tac airport and Bozmania went officially bonkers. I made a poster with *Playboy* centerfold Ava Fabian that outsold Jim McMahon's poster faster than you can say Taco Bell. We had ten thousand T-shirts for sale the day I arrived in Seattle and we sold out all of them and went through sixty thousand more besides.

My company—44 Boz, Inc.—owns the rights to my name (including nicknames) and my likeness, so I'm the only one who can put out a T-shirt with me on it. In the first year alone, we had to send out about twenty-five cease-and-desist orders. One of 'em was to this one knucklehead who might go down as the most two-faced person in history. When I was saying no to Seattle all that time, he was selling these BOZ-BUSTERS baseball hats in town. But when I signed, all that changed. "Now that he's on the *Good Ship Lollipop*," this guy told the paper, "I'll get hats that say something else." And he did. And people say *I'm* greedy. At least I don't sell my opinion, up or down, left or right, depending on how the stock market is turning.

Somebody came out with those signs you hang in your window: BOZ ON BOARD. I had to stop playing golf on my days off because every time I'd hit my drive, some kids would jump out of the bushes and steal my ball. One time I got pulled over for a traffic ticket and while I was waiting to get written up (Seattle isn't Norman—yet), I was listening to an FM station and next thing you know they're saying, "The Boz is getting pulled over for a traffic ticket." I looked up and there was their helicopter. Now you know what I'm up against. Even from five hundred feet straight up, I'm unmistakable.

In a matter of weeks, Seattle set me up royal. I developed a great relationship with a Seattle-based Chevrolet dealer, Lee Johnson, who gave me a brand-new Corvette to drive, which I thought was a nice touch, since I'm so close with the good folks at GM. Can't you see the main guy in Detroit when he hears about it? "You did *what*?!?" An apartment complex gave me an apartment to stay in for free. A restaurant I liked offered to give me all my meals for free—even delivered—if I came in there once in a while. A beer company offered to drop off beer now and again. (Who am I to refuse?) A stereo store gave me a huge big-screen TV. Practically everything I had was free, from the furniture to the walls to the pictures that hung on them. It was almost depressing. What's the point of signing for $11 million if you don't have to spend 11¢? Oh well, my mother told me it's rude to turn people down. The NFL ride, I decided, was almost as cushy as college.

But the best part of being in Seattle was the fact that finally—nine months since the last time I'd been in pads and a hundred and sixty hours of work behind everybody else—I was a football player again.

At my first practice I was introduced to all the players in the locker room. I got some friendly handshakes and a lot of "F__ you too" stares. The offensive linemen were funny, though. They said they were all changing their last names to Bosworth so they could get some publicity. Then our center, Kani Kauahi from Hawaii, decided to call his haircut The Coz.

"How come, Kani?"

"Coz I've had it for a long time."

One guy that I knew hated me, because I'd heard him on TV, was Greg Gaines. Every time I heard somebody ripping me, it was Gaines, saying, "Why do people keep talking about this dude? He isn't even here yet." I said to myself, "Me and this sumbitch are going to have it out." I decided not to put it off, so that very first day I asked somebody, "Where's Gaines?"

They took me to the back of the training room and there was Gaines, smoking a cigarette, chilling out where nobody could see him. Mr. Cool. And do you know what terrible, disgusting thing he said to me?

"Hey, how you doing? Glad you're here."

That's it. As things turned out, I was closer to him than almost anybody on the whole team.

One reason I liked Gainesey is that he treated me like a human being. Everybody else in Seattle—the press and the fans—treated me like I was going to start out the first season of my career and make everybody forget Lawrence Taylor ever existed. No, that's wrong. They expected it after the first *game*.

Expectations were so high in Seattle that I could play for ten years and never meet them. They wanted me to make every tackle, every sack, and score every touchdown. And here I was, getting handed a playbook about the size of the Encyclopaedia Britannica. We didn't even *have* a playbook at OU.

I was totally lost at every practice for a long time.

Yet at the end of every practice, there'd be crowds of reporters waiting to talk to me. I kept asking myself, "What in the hell can they want to talk to me about?" And the answer was always, "The same thing as yesterday."

REPORTERS: "How are you doing out there?"

ME: "I don't know. I haven't been in on a single play yet."

REPORTERS: "Are you just figuring out what you're doing?"

ME: "Yeah, I need some Rustoleum. Got any?"

And forty more minutes like that. It was outrageous. I was losing my mind. I wanted to tap my heels together three times and get my ass back to Kansas.

I was spending my off days and nights with our defensive coordinator, Tom (Top Cat) Catlin, The Most Serious Man in the World, trying to absorb the playbook. Those were real hilarious times. Catlin never cracked a smile the whole time.

And then, to make matters worse—to make matters a whole gaddamn *lot* worse—I got the number I've worn since high school jerked off my back.

It actually started the very first day I got there. I went down to get my practice jersey and they said, "What number do you want?"

"What do you mean what number do I want? Give me 44, like I've always had."

"You can't have 44. League rules. You're a linebacker and linebackers have to wear numbers between 50 and 70. We'll give you 55."

I walked right back upstairs and right into McCormack's office and said, "Deal's off."

I explained the whole thing to him. (1) I'd played

as 44 since I was a kid; (2) I'm extremely superstitious. I couldn't even imagine stepping on the field
without wearing 44; (3) I had a lot of money tied up
in 44. My company is called 44, Boz, Inc. And we'd
signed a deal to market our own line of clothes and
sunglasses called 44 Blues. Now what? I'm supposed to change it to 55 Blues? "Yeah, this is Brian.
Can you do me a favor? Can you just cross out all
those 44s on all those jeans and shirts and shoes and
write in 55?"

McCormack jumped right on it, got them to give
me 44, but two weeks later, when we were playing
the St. Louis Cardinals in our first preseason game—
my first game as a pro—Pete Rozelle 86'd my 44.
Why? *Why?* Because players need to stay within their
number limits. That's why. That's how come Karl
Mecklenburg of the Denver Broncos—a linebacker—
wears 77. That's how come Todd Christensen of the
Raiders—a tight end who is supposed to wear a
number in the 80s—wears 46.

"Well," some muckity-muck at the NFL said,
"that's because they came *into* the league at a different position and were allowed to keep their number when they changed."

"Fine," I said. "I'm coming into the league as a
monster defensive back. Give me 44."

But the league nixed that idea. Said that they knew
I was a linebacker. I was so pissed off about it that
I wore a 44 decal on my shoes and on the seat of
my pants later on in the year in a game against Green
Bay. The refs made me remove them on the second
play of the game. I told the reporters, "Looks like
lawsuit number 28B."

And it was. We took it to court—all on our own,

of course. For some reason, the Seahawks, who had said they'd stand behind me, never stood behind me. When it came time to go to court, they wimped out. In fact, in McCormack's sworn statement he said, "I don't recall telling Brian that we'd allow him to wear 44." Hmmmm. How strange. I wonder how I got this picture with me, him, and John Nordstrom, the Seahawks' owner, in it, all holding up a 44 jersey with my name on it? In fact, McCormack brought that very jersey to that restaurant in Los Colinas and held it up all of a sudden for dramatic value. I wonder if McCormack recalls *that*.

So we went to court without help and the judge, Judge Clueless, decided not to rule on my case.

"Mr. Bosworth, my wife solved this case for me last night," he said. "You've obviously won on all three points, but I have no past case to rule on."

Read that as: "Mr. Bosworth, my wife says I don't have any balls. And I certainly don't have the balls to set a precedent for once in my life. I don't want to ruin my record in case I'm wrong. So I'm going to puss out altogether."

I wanted to say, "Well, give your wife the robe or give me back the $25,000 I paid for the court time, asshole!"

Every time after that, whenever I'd try to wear 44 on my body, Rozelle would have a hemorrhoid and call somebody to get me to get rid of it. I wore a 44 BLUES logo on my shoes, a legit logo, just like Nike or Reebok or anybody else's logo—and they made me take it off. I call that restraint of trade. And when the owners met after my rookie season, one of the things they turned down was letting me have 44. Actually, I don't know if they know *what* they turned down. They all start out in the morning at those meetings drinking that Black Label Scotch and by five o'clock they're approving moving a franchise to El Salvador.

I don't know what Rozelle's problem is. Maybe when he was forty-four—about fifty years ago—he had a bad year. Maybe that's when the rates at the tanning booth went up or something. Then again, maybe I do know what Rozelle's problem is. When I first came into the league, the NFL wanted to co-venture a deal. They wanted to license me and my name and my likeness. We told them to stick it. We knew they needed us more than we need them. A whole helluva lot of people will buy a poster of me that never even *heard* of the Seattle Seahawks. I'm sure that pissed off Pete because it could have made the league some serious money. Since I came to Seattle, the Seahawks have passed the Cowboys as the team that sells the most NFL Property items— T-shirts, jerseys, helmets. This was based on a chain of stores across the country—Spectathlete—that sells the stuff. That means Seattle is the most popular team in the country. Spectathlete also said that "a large share of the Seahawk sales have been attributed to purchases of a jersey bearing the number 55." Take that, Pete.

So maybe because I wouldn't go along with their deal, Turtle Face has decided to step on me. Doesn't want Boz getting an upper hand on him. Cost The Man some money. The Man could've used some money for a face-lift. Pete's got more chins than Divine did.

The league is so hypocritical that way. After all that happened that year, they called me after the season was over to go to London to spread good cheer about the NFL during the Super Bowl. And guess who sponsored it? Budweiser. I went, but I don't know why. And yet the NFL has a league rule against players doing ads for any alcohol or cigarette company. Of course, if the money is going to the league, then it's a different story, right? Just like it's a different story that the NFL now has those idiotic "Budweiser kickoffs" now too. A kid watching at home thinks we all stand around and go, "Hey, let's suck down a Bud before this kickoff, okay?"

That's when I figured something out about the NFL. It's just the NCAA in nicer suits.

CHAPTER
14

They Shoot Linebackers, Don't They?

Despite our being blown out of the playoffs in the first round . . . and despite the fact that our defense gave up more yards than Refrigerator Perry's shirt-maker . . . and despite the fact that it took some of my teammates a while to accept me for who I am (which, I admit, takes some time) . . . and despite the fact that I didn't talk to my good buddies, the journalists of Seattle, for the entire regular season . . . my first season as a professional football player sometimes *was* a hoot. Any season in which you get to hit John Elway six times as hard as the law allows is a good season.

But the problem was, I was lied to and when I get lied to I'm not a happy camper. From the beginning the Seahawks told me I would play strong-inside linebacker. For you novice football fans and sports-writers out there, it's the position I'd played since high school. It's the position I won two Butkus Awards playing and led OU in tackles from for three straight years. It's an *impact* linebacker's position and, God knows, I love impacts. You're on the strong side—the side the offense has their tight end on—so that means they come your way 80 percent of the time on runs.

But on the first day of practice with the Seahawks,

I ran in there at strong-inside linebacker and they said, "Hold it a minute . . . You're a *weak*-inside linebacker." That's sort of like the difference between being in the front seat at a drive-in with a gorgeous girl or being in the trunk with your little brother. All you do on weak-inside linebacker is get over to the other side and clean up plays. The ball-carrier is usually down or at least in somebody's arms by the time you get there and your job is to sweep up. "Everybody okay here? Great." It's like always backing up third base.

Weak-inside linebacker sucks larvae, but they put me there, they said, because it takes a lot of brains. Weak makes all the calls on defense. They kept Freddie Young at the strong side. They either didn't think Freddie was smart enough to learn weakside or they didn't think I was good enough to play strongside. If the second reason is true, then somebody just blew $11 million. If that's all they wanted me for, I became the highest-paid mop-up man this side of Dan Quisenberry.

When Catlin told me where I'd be playing, I wanted to just walk out the door. Here I'd orchestrated it so that I could sign with any team in the league and the team I pick sticks me in right field.

"Funny how all along, through all the meetings, Knox and McCormack always had me at strong," I told Catlin.

"Well, we're going to try Freddie there," Catlin said.

"I wouldn't have signed if I'd have known this."

I was pissed out of my mind, but, seeing no way out of it, I decided to do my best. That's where they wanted me, I'd do it. They were crazy, but I'd do it. Good boy, Fido.

And once I started doing it, I learned one thing about pro ball right away. Nobody pushes your hot button for you. It's not like in college. You've got to get jacked up on your own. That's what I found out after we played St. Louis (now Phoenix) in that first exhibition game. (Pete Rozelle hates it when you call it an "exhibition" game. He wants you to say "pre-season" game.) I had no fun that game. There was no emotion. I learned pretty quickly. The NFL is not an adventure, it's a job.

I had absolutely no clue what I was doing at my job. Hell, I'd only been in the league *four days*. So, of course, the writers reamed me a new one. One guy wrote something like "When the Cardinals ran a play up the middle, we expected to hear a sonic boom. Instead, all we heard was deafening silence." They wanted me to *own* this league the first game I played. But they never mentioned a word about how the other rookies were playing. There was no pressure on them. They were expected to start slowly until they learned. But me? I had to earn my $11 million right then and there or I was a fraud.

So imagine my surprise to hear Catlin telling me I'd start the season opener against Denver. The only reason I didn't refuse was that I dearly wanted to plant an elbow in Elway's earhole. Some Denver reporters asked me if I'd hit Elway even if it meant a yellow flag. I danced around the question. I said I was fixing on playing with abandon and you can't play with abandon if you're thinking of penalties all the time. When Knox heard that, he got in my kitchen. He called me into his office and told me that wasn't Seahawk football. Then he told the reporters, "Brian Bosworth was wrong. That's the amateur in him coming through."

So much for Knox promising not to muzzle me.

Because of all that, the scene at Mile High Stadium for the Denver game was as wild as anything I'd ever been a part of. The Denver fans were screaming profanities, spitting tobacco and beer at me, and grinning their black teeth off. And some of the men were just as bad. (Drum cymbals.) Then again, there were a lot of people yelling for me to kick Elway's ass. And I still think it's funny that it was Elway who got death threats, not me. I guess some people love Johnny Dangerously as much as me.

The fans were all over my butt, but I was the one that got the last laugh. About ten thousand of them had on T-shirts with my face in a circle with a diagonal line through it. Like the *Ghostbusters* symbol. They said something like WHAT'S A BOZ WORTH? NOTHING! And BAN THE BOZ on the back. But if they had looked inside the shirt at the little tag that said 44 BOZ, INC., those hosebags would have realized they just paid fifteen dollars for a shirt made by my company. We gave all the profits to the Children's Hospital. We just wanted to prove how oxygen-deprived Denver fans are.

Their players aren't exactly MENSA members either. Two plays into the game, one of Denver's big brave Elway protectors, center Billy Bryan, cheap-shotted me from behind after the whistle. The fans went crazy, but I just said, "Fine. I love it. Don't you ever turn your back to me the rest of the day, you son of a bitch." I got him back later with a knee to the throat. I'll bet he had to take nothing but liquids for days.

I got to Elway on a rollout on that first series. He was scrambling to his right like he does, thinking he could make it to the sideline, and I got in a great hit on him. Then I yelled right up his nose, *"I'm your worst nightmare, Blankety-blank."* That sort of stunned him. I remember the next time we played them, in Seattle, he was ready with his reply. I hit him and he jumped up and screamed, *"Aaaaaaa-aghaaaaawrghh!!!"*

I told him, "At least I use words, home boy."

I have to admit it, though. He was great that first game and they beat us bad. But we came back the next week and kicked Kansas City's ass, a game I will recall fondly because I coldcocked the Chiefs' quarterback, Bill Kenney, so hard that when they turned him over his eyes were rolled up in his head and his mouth was bleeding. I must say, Mike Tyson couldn't have done a better job. I whispered into his ear, "Jesus, Bill. You better not get up because if you have to throw another pass, your ass will be out of the game." I mean, he was ugly before, but now he was really ugly.

I realized after what Bryan did to me that I wasn't going to be on a whole lot of NFL players' Christmas card lists. They were either jealous of the contract or the name or my handsome looks. (Ahem.) Which is fine. But I never thought guys would start making stuff up about me. After this game, one of the Chiefs' offensive linemen, Mark Adickes, said that he helped on a touchdown by "faking the run block and then knocking over The Boz." But when reporters told him I wasn't anywhere near the play,

Adickes just grinned and said, "This is my story and I'll tell it any way I want." Bad enough I've got guys hitting me after the whistle. Now I've got guys hitting me in their dreams.

Anyway, I was starting to feel a little better about what I was doing when the union announced we were on strike. Nice.

That was the start of a lot of trouble. I guess some of the players got upset with me because, instead of staying on the picket line, which went pretty strong until the guys had polished off all the donuts the wives brought the first day, I went and had fun. I went to New York to host MTV for a while. That was a kick, just sitting there and talking about music and videos. I'm an MTV freak anyway. I sat there with Julie Brown and drank beer out of a coffee cup while we taped it. The *National Sports Review* said I was "some kind of Dick Clark from another universe." I like it. I give it a 97. Good beat and easy to dance to.

Then I went to L.A. to do "The Tonight Show" with guest host Garry Shandling, who is a real drip. The guy was so insecure about what he was doing that during the commercials he'd say, "Well, what can I ask you next? Give me something to ask you next." Still, I was having fun and I was working out hard during the days. Wasn't hurting anybody. Or so I thought.

Some guys on the team thought, since I was the most visible person on the team, I should be out front carrying a sandwich board in front of the Seahawk offices. Why? I didn't have a bitch with the Seahawks. None of us did. The Seahawks treat us like kings. We should've been picketing Rozelle's office if we were going to picket. Besides, how much credibility does a guy who just signed for $11 million have walking a picket line? What was I supposed to do? Carry a sign that said: MANAGEMENT UNFAIR TO MILLIONAIRES? The guy at home would just go, "Oh, give me a break." I think I did more good staying *off* the line.

But Jacob Green, our six-foot-three, 252-pound defensive end, didn't think so and we almost exchanged fist sandwiches over it. We were holding a team meeting at Mike Tice's deli and having a few beers. Our wise and wonderful representatives, Gene Upshaw and the Players' Disunion, were about to cave in and we were trying to decide when we should cross the line.

"Hey, look," I said. "I need every day I can get on the practice field. I think we should go in on Wednesday."

Jacob jumped in my face. "Well, maybe you should've thought of that before you did all those TV appearances. You should've been here with us!"

"Wait a minute," I said. "I went to five practices during the strike and I only saw you at two of them."

We were nose-to-nose and some guys stepped between us. We were both half-drunk and very frustrated. He said he was sorry and so did I. I'm glad. I don't think I'd want to see what either one of us would've looked like after a fight like that.

I respected Jacob because he didn't cross the line, even though he was losing some serious money. I didn't respect guys like our kicker Norm Johnson, whom we now call Scab. He crossed. So did Freddie Young. My gut feeling was that we should *win* as a team and stay out as a team. I lost total respect for those players who crossed. Steve Largent crossed too, but he has a kid with cerebral palsy and his doctor bills were outrageous. But those other guys, like our quarterback, Jeff Kemp, had no balls. The union is only as tight as the players and those guys might just have ruined it for everybody from here on in.

By the time the strike was over, four weeks later, it was like having to start training camp again. And I never had training camp to begin with. Plus, the vibes sucked. We were a divided team. Half of the guys were still pissed about the strike. The other half were pissed off at the guys who crossed the line. And I think all of us were bitter because we'd stayed out for no reason and lost stacks of dough. And you know me. I need every penny to sue my man Pete.

Footballwise, our scab team went 2–1, so we weren't hurt, and then we won our next two—over the Raiders in L.A. (in front of what looked to me like an entire stadium of illegal aliens) and then the Vikings at home. We were suddenly 5–2 and looking good. Then we did something stupid: lost to the Jets, which was almost as stupid as what I did before the game. I missed curfew by fifteen lousy minutes on *Saturday* night before a *Monday* game. Don't ask me why we have curfew two nights before a game, but we do. And because my damn cabbie turned the wrong way out of the Lincoln Tunnel I was fifteen minutes late. I got gouged for $500. The next morning I went downstairs and Knox had a grin on his face the size of the Brooklyn Bridge.

"Well, you sure did buy a lot of basketballs for the Boys' Club in Seattle last night," he said. "Don't you feel better?"

"Yeah, Coach. I feel like Mother Teresa."

It wasn't so much the money that pissed me off, it was that I would've been fined $500 if I was fifteen minutes late or five hours late. If I knew I was going to be fined, I'd have stayed out and gotten my $500 worth. I was only slightly brightened by what I saw Monday as we pulled into Giants Stadium for the game. The marquee said: TONIGHT: THE JETS VS. THE BOZ AND THE SEAHAWKS. Now *that's* billing.

We won our next two games—Green Bay, which I thought was the hardest-hitting game I'd been in yet, and San Diego—both at home. Now we were 7–3 and people were calling us the best thing to happen to Seattle since umbrellas. But that's when the sky fell in.

That's when the world starting jumping on the "Ban the Boz" bandwagon. It started with a Monday night loss to the Raiders at home the next week. An outfielder for the Kansas City Royals went nuts on us. Bo Jackson ran through us like we were first base and he was on his way to a triple. He gained 220 yards—one went for 90 yards—and one time he just flat freight-trained my ass over for a touchdown. It was my own fault. He came up inside and I didn't know if he was going to cut it back and try to run it inside or go outside. So I hesitated for a second and that's all it took. I wasn't set and he knocked my ass over. I'm sure they ran that one back a few times in the ABC booth.

That wasn't bad, but losing to Pittsburgh and the planet's worst quarterback, Mark Malone, the next week was worse.

I played lousy and to make things worse, it was Story Hour again. This time it was about my headband that I wear with a long tail down the back. It keeps sweat out of my eyes. The tail was just to do something different. When I do something different, something I know some people aren't going to like, it puts pressure on me to perform. I like that. I *need* that. Well, these two Steeler goons told reporters they pulled the tail off my head and took it to the sideline. One of those guys said he even twirled it on the sidelines. But the only "tail" was the one they were telling. I never lost the headband. I had it on at the start of the game and at the end. Those guys either had somebody else's tail or they hadn't gotten any real "tail" for so long, they were hallucinating.

Anyway, that's when the shit hit the fan. When we got back to Seattle, we stopped in a favorite dispensary of drink and we were having a few beers and Dave Krieg jumps in my face, which was becoming a popular place to jump on this team.

"Why do you always have to be different?" he said.

"I don't know. Why do you always have to be normal?"

"Why do you have to cut your practice jerseys and wear sunglasses under your helmet?"

"Because I like to. Why are you the way you are?"

"It's all a show, isn't it?"

"Yeah. It *is* a show until game time. Then I'm the most serious son of a bitch on the field. Do you have a problem with that?"

"Yeah . . ."

By now we're about to get into family histories. But nobody got punched. We left growling at each other. He just didn't understand me yet. Hell yes, I'll do anything to alleviate the boredom and I don't give a damn what you think of it, but when I play, I play at only full speed. The other stuff doesn't matter. He's got to see past the side stuff, but he couldn't yet. Just like the press couldn't either. After that game the writers were calling for my benching, guys who've never played football in their life. Guys weighing 163 pounds with 20–400 vision and biceps the size of bug bites thinking they're Don Shula. Some of these guys, the biggest sweat they ever work up is putting their underwear on real fast. And they're saying, "Bench the Boz." *How special.* Who needs the facts? Let's just write whatever fills up our little two-page sports sections. That's the size our sports sections are in Seattle: two pages, front and back. It kills me. And three quarters of that is lawn mower ads.

The facts, if they only knew them, were simple enough. For that year, we gave up more than 400 yards in total offense two times and more than 500 yards two times, which must be the worst in the league. Our defense ranked twenty-second in the league. Here I was, a guy who used to get out the razor blades in college if we gave up positive rushing yardage, now giving up yardage like it was frequent-flier mileage.

One reason our defense didn't work is that we didn't have enough guys who were willing to sacrifice individual goals to make it work as a team. We had two or three guys who were too worried about what their stats were—whether they were going to reach all their contract incentive clauses or not, whether they were going to be All-Pro or not—to play unselfishly. So they'd leave their area and go for the sack or the glory hit.

That bullshit looks good in the press box, but for every time they get a great sack and the crowd goes wild, there's five times when they get burned like toast and the guy gets fifteen yards in the hole they just abandoned. The fans can't tell and it doesn't show up in the All-Pro picks. The way the All-Pro teams are selected in the NFL is a total joke anyway. You want to know how we voted for All-Pro that year? Kenny Easley walked in the room, called the meeting to order, wrote down the names he thought should be All-Pro on the chalkboard, and we voted for them. He didn't put up any other names on the board. There were no other choices. Whatever Easley wanted, we were supposed to vote for. "Is democratic process, comrade." Screw that. I voted for guys that had been retired for five years. I think two of them actually made the Pro Bowl!

I'm not trying to say I didn't have a part in giving up all those ungodly yards. I did. But at least put me in my position and see how many we give up.

There were more coming distractions. Like a knuckle-head, I'd given an interview to a guy from the Washington *Post*, Michael Wilbon, and he caught me when I was a little depressed about all this. I told him exactly how I felt.

"So far, I've probably had zero amount of fun playing the game," I told him. I said the three months I'd been in Seattle were three of the most uncomfortable months of my whole life. Football was supposed to be the one thing I loved to do more than anything in life and the people around me were making me hate it. Plus, I said, I didn't have a lot of friends on the team yet, only a handful of guys. We were still feeling each other out.

It was all true. I mean, I was still trying to cope with how much fame and pressure I suddenly had on me after the lottery thing. Plus, I was depressed about never being able to even leave my apartment. It's hard enough on anybody moving to a new city, taking a new job, having to make all new friends—without the whole world staring down in on you, asking you what you eat for breakfast every day. All I was trying to tell people in that article was to scale down their expectations, to treat me as a human being. Don't send me to school and then on the first day give me a final exam.

I'm not a robot. I was down. I spent a whole lot of money on long-distance that week calling my two favorite coaches—Russ Widener, my linebacker coach from high school, and Coach Gibbs from OU. I had to talk to *somebody*. I remember saying, "Why can't I just play football? Why do they have to bring money into it? Why can't we all just have fun playing it like it's supposed to be played? Why does everybody have to worry about how much I make a year or what I'm wearing during the game or whether my socks are pulled up all the way?"

Well, the *Post* article went over in Seattle like acid rain. Stupid me. I should've known not to be honest. The town thought I meant I hated Seattle and the team. My teammates thought I hated them.

The whole city was so concerned they decided to take it upon themselves to solve my problem. This one TV station had one of those phone-in-your-vote questions that they do instead of actually bringing you the news, and they broke all existing records on me. They asked, "What should Boz do?" They had something like forty-six thousand calls in six hours. Twenty-nine percent said I should go home, 26 percent said give it time, 25 percent said stop whining, and 20 percent said speak out more. So I conducted my own poll: One hundred percent of people who call TV phone-in polls don't have enough to do.

Everybody took it like I was sitting around my apartment holding two cyanide capsules and a glass of water. That wasn't the deal at all. He just caught me on a bad day. But I guess it upset some of my teammates. One reporter quoted Jeff Bryant, one of our defensive ends, as saying that we still had team unity despite "one bad apple." As my man Keith Butler would put it, it don't take no rocket scientist to figure out he meant me.

I decided to get it all out in the open. I talked to as many players as I could about it and told them what I really meant. I told them it was no reflection on them. I just was pissed about my position. I even asked Jeff about the apple thing and he said he never said anything like that. Happiness was back in the Dome.

I mean, I really do like a lot of my teammates: Minkman (Sam Merriman, a linebacker); Gainesey; Crane (Bryant, because when he spreads his arms, he looks like a big crane); Butler, who is my main guru and chief good ol' Tennessee boy; Steve Largent, our All-Galaxy wide receiver who everybody calls Yoda because that's who he looks like; our nose guard Joe (Air) Nash. We call him Air Nash because when he jumps you can just about get a gum wrapper between his shoes and the ground.

Some guys, of course, I'm not ready to pick out

china patterns with yet. Brian Millard, an offensive linemen, and I fight like cats and dogs. He's always wearing one of those BOZ-BUSTERS hats around or BAN THE BOZ T-shirts. I guess he thinks it's funny, but the joke got old after the first week.

Me and Knox are a different deal. We're not real close, but we're not enemies either. I respect him. He's got eyes like one of those Uncle Sam posters. No matter where you go, he always is looking right at you. But I like him. He's stuck up for me. One time he said in a press conference, "Everybody talks about how different Bosworth is. Well, he graduated in four years. *That's different.*" He had a 3.3 grade-point average. *That's different.* He's a 248-pound guy who can run a 4.59. *That's different.*

So when all this Washington *Post* stuff hit, I went into his office and talked it over with him. He said he understood some of the frustrations. He just chalked it up to experience. That was cool.

Anyway, after a week as bad as that, something good had to happen and, luckily, here came my favorite tackling dummy, Elway. Denver came to the Dome and we stomped 'em. I took out every pissed-off emotion I had on Mr. Ed that night. I rattled him the whole game. He thinks he's a great scrambler, but he's not fast enough to get away from me. I chased him down. I busted his ass four times. If I'd had a gun that night, I'd have killed him. I didn't care. Send me to Attica. It would have been worth it.

"Whatju in for, man?"

"Killed the human Ken doll, John Elway."

"Gimme five!"

Now we were 8–5 and we still had a chance to

make the playoffs. All we had to do was go to Chicago and beat the Bears. Sort of like saying all you've got to do is go to Philadelphia and break into the Mint. The Bears, even without Jim McMahon, were *good*. But so what? We smoked 'em. I thought I played terrible, but the rest of the world thought I played great because I tore the ball out of Neil Anderson's hands on a sweep play (I was cleaning up, of course). I was lying on the ground and Air Nash was next to me and I was screaming, "Man, Joe! I got the damn ball! I got the damn ball!"

And Joe is screaming, "Well get your ass up and run with it then!"

Sounded like a good idea so I sort of Frankensteined it down the sideline thirty-five yards to the one. One lousy yard away from my first collegiate or pro touchdown. Mike Tomczak, the Chicago quarterback, a guy who weighs maybe 180 pounds, tripped me up. May you get gum decay for that, Tomczak.

They even gave me AFC Defensive Player of the Week for that game. Everything was clean. We were 9–5 and all we had to do was beat Kansas City and we'd be home for the first round of the playoffs. And there's no place like Dome.

But on the plane out to Kansas City we found out Pittsburgh had lost. That meant we'd clinched a wildcard berth. Well, that isn't what we wanted. We wanted to be *home* for the playoffs. But it was too late. Right then, the moment they told us, I could feel this real big letdown. Right then, I knew we were going to lose. I wish they'd have kept us all in some soundproof booth so we'd never have known. Instead, the whole mood of the team changed. The pressure was off. Everybody on the plane was saying, "What are you going to do with your six thousand?" That's what the minimum is for being a wild-card team: $6,000. I hope they all enjoyed it because we lost that game and had to go to Houston for the playoff game and lost there too. That was the worst $6,000 I ever won.

Still, that Houston game was the most fun I had that year. For one thing, everybody that came to the game got a free pair of very cheapo earrings—a reference to my ear apparel, I guess. For another thing, the Oilers were the dirtiest team we played all season and I liked it. I like it when you can't turn your back for a minute, whistle or no whistle. Houston guard Mike Munchak held me like I was his fiancée. He ripped two jerseys off me and I hadn't had one ripped all year.

And guess who was on the other side, beating me again and loving it? Alonzo Highsmith, that's who.

And I still couldn't think of anything to scream at him.

CHAPTER
15

The Last Picture Show

When somebody twenty-three writes an autobiography, like I just did, most of his life hasn't even happened yet. At least I hope that's true. Unless I pick another fight with Jacob Green and he closes out my dance card sooner than I'd hoped.

I know that I'm probably lucky to have even made it to twenty-three as it is, but I have big plans for the rest of my life. For one thing, I've never had the pleasure of ripping the eyelashes off His Ineptness, OU President Frank Horton. I've never hit a guy so hard that they have to surgically remove my forearm from his ribs.

I know one thing: I *will* play football until they have to bring a crane out to the field and hoist me off. And I'll never have another season as frustrating as my rookie season.

Now if I can just get Catlin to rely on me the way I want to be relied on, the way Gibbs did, the way my father did before that. As time goes by, I think he will. I want the defense to be built around me like it was at OU. I want all the pressure on me. That's when I play the best. It makes options for other guys, opens up doors for them to freelance, stops pesky rodent offenses and *kills them dead*.

The thing is, this team is loaded with talent. We have more talent than anybody in the AFC, including the Elways. We should be in the Super Bowl, not those donkeys. And we will be too. I want to be in bunches of them. I can't imagine playing a career and never going to the Super Bowl. If I did that, I'd call my career a total waste. If you can tell me that's what's going to happen, I'll quit right now and become a whole-life insurance salesman or something.

The Super Bowl is one thing. The Pro Bowl is another. I don't think I'll ever be popular enough to make it to the Pro Bowl because the players vote on the Pro Bowl and too many players aren't smart enough to see that I've helped them. Anytime one player's salary goes way up, the rest have to follow behind. I pushed back the envelope on the damn owners. But a lot of players can't see that. All they see is a haircut and a lot of tax-free bonds and they don't like it. It doesn't really make a difference to me. I know what I'm about. I don't care if the players like me or hate me. They still have to play me and block me. And, if I hit them, listen to me.

Football is my stage right now, but when I'm done with football I'll need a new stage. I have a need to be onstage, just like an actor or a singer or performer. I love to perform for people. Only when I perform now—unlike Whitney Houston or somebody—half the people get mad and half get deliriously happy. The problem my rookie year was that, sometimes, the half that got mad were our own fans.

. . . I'm taking acting lessons. I moved to Los Angeles after my rookie season so I could start. I've heard Jack Nicholson is losing sleep over it. I got a chance to try out my new acting skills when I taped a couple of commercials for Gillette in New York. I liked how they turned out. I only wanted to do ads for a few big companies and Gillette seemed right. I wanted to look cool. I didn't want to be some big goofball sucking up cereal with milk dripping down my chin. I don't know who would do those commercials anyway. "Look, Mom. That's me. Slobbering all over myself. Isn't it great?"

You've got to respect yourself and not sell yourself like a human billboard. I don't do any appearances anywhere—for any amount of money. I was offered $25,000 to come down and answer questions at some dinner—fifteen, twenty minutes, tops—but I didn't do it. I don't sign autographs at malls and I don't hang around the local car dealership, giving away wristbands with each test drive. When a company signs me, like Gillette, they get something that not everybody has. It's sort of a rare public appearance and it takes on kind of an event feel to it. Does that sound like I think I'm Michael Jackson?

But that makes sense in the wallet too. I heard Vinny Testaverde made about $250,000 doing endorsements his rookie year. Vinny's a great player and all, but I could make that in a week handing out cookies at Mrs. Fields.

Commercials are easy for me. That's why I think movies will be easy too. Hell, I've spent 93 percent of my life in front of a camera anyway. I might as well get paid to do it for once. I can sit there on Carson or Letterman and be as natural and normal as if I was talking to you in my living room. (But I better not catch you in my living room.)

Besides, I like the way they treat you in Hollywood. They've always got limousines for you. People in L.A. take limos everywhere. "Boris, be a dear and bring the limo 'round. I must procure a package of cigarettes at the 7-Eleven." I love limos. They're the only place I can really stretch out my legs. For "The Tonight Show," they picked me up at my hotel at three in the afternoon in a limo about the size of a par-five golf hole. We didn't even have to be to the studio until five. The driver's only job was to make sure I got there.

"You want to go to the studio now?" he said.

"Nah," I said. "Tell you what. Let's go to the liquor store and get a six of those big sixteen-ounce beers and you just drive around and show me the city."

I do believe that was the first six-pack of sixteen-ounce Buds ever drank in that limo without the use of Waterford crystal.

I see myself in movies as sort of an Arnold Schwarzenegger with a sense of humor. A guy who cracks jokes while he's cracking people's skulls. And unlike all of his commando movies, mine would actually have *plots*. And you'd actually be able to *understand* what I'm saying. Comin' after you, Arnie.

Of course the problem with making a living in Hollywood is that you have to hang around with Hollywood people. They're not all bad, I guess. I'm friends with the guy who plays McGyver on TV, Richard Dean Anderson. We went to the Denver–Giants Super Bowl together. I had the great pleasure of seeing John Elway do his yearly Stupor Bowl act.

But for the most part, Hollywood people give me the creeps. All they want to do is talk about themselves and do coke. I went to this one Hollywood birthday party and as soon as I walked in the door,

I knew I'd made a mistake. Not only were there hookers everywhere, there was enough cocaine to pave Colombia. And Hollywood people can't just do it themselves. They want *you* to do it. And if you don't do it, they get pissed. So after about five minutes of that, I found a bedroom, closed the door, and turned on the TV. And about ten minutes later, somebody came in right behind me. Henry Winkler. I guess he can't handle being around drugs any more than I can. He said, "Well, The Fonz meets The Boz." And we both stayed in there the whole night, just talking. I started to feel like Ralph Malph after a while.

When I get so sick of Hollywood people that I can't make movies anymore, I'm going to start spending all my money. I'm going to buy an island, an entire island, and kick everybody else the hell off it and invite only who I want. What do you think Maui would go for?

I'll build a dream house on it. After years of sleeping in puny hotel beds, I'll have a bed the size of two kings. I'll have a shower as big or maybe slightly larger than the Dome in Seattle. I'll have speakers in every room. I'll have a bunch of wild animals on the island, lions and bears—and not the Detroit and Chicago kind. Maybe I'll invite Pete and Elway and some of my pals from the NCAA and Horton. I'll lock the door and let them fend for themselves with my furry friends. Maybe they'll eat each other.

I know one thing I *don't* want to do on that island is grow old. I can't stand the thought of being old. I don't want to be an old prunehead walking around, growling at all the kids, my mind so closed up you can't squeeze anything in it that didn't happen before 1979.

When I start to feel old, I don't want to continue living. I define "feeling old" as when you're just sitting around, going, "*Sheeee-ut*. I can't do this no more. I can't do that no more. I never have sex anymore. I might as well call it a goddamn day."

Maybe that's how I'll feel when I'm fifty. Then again, the government says the life span of the average NFL football player is fifty-two. Maybe I won't have to worry about it. Maybe I won't feel old until I'm seventy. But whenever it is, I'm offing myself. I'm serious. I don't know how I'll do it, but I will. Maybe I'll just stare at a picture of Brian Millard until my skull caves in.

Maybe my kids will make me feel young. I know I want kids. Uh-oh. All over the country, sirens just went off in people's heads. *"The Boz?! Reproducing?!"* Yeah, the Boz reproducing. I want a boy, just like my dad wanted a boy. I want someone to make me proud. I don't care what he does. He can be an interior decorator, for all I care. Just so he does something and likes it. I'll spoil him. And I'll teach him that it doesn't matter what people think of you, as long as you can look at yourself in the mirror eye-to-eye. Because people are going to think what they want to think, see what they want to see. Once I learned that truth, my life was a lot simpler.

I'll also teach him to thank God for what he has. I didn't do that for a long time. Not until one rainy night in Norman during my sophomore year in college.

We were all meeting at a bar, having a few beverages, shooting some pool. Two of us weren't there yet: Keith Stansbury and Andre Johnson. Both were good friends of mine and both were great players. Keith was a safety and Andre was a cornerbacker. Keith was a lock to be a first-round choice at the end of that year.

All of a sudden we heard a sickening crash outside. I ran outside and saw Keith's red 300-ZX totaled against a telephone pole. It was a wet night and they were going too fast. They hit some railroad tracks and flew a little bit and when they came down they lost control and slammed it into the pole. As soon as I saw it, I crumbled to my knees and cried.

Keith was pinned inside. Andre crawled out. They lived but their careers were ruined. Both of them crushed both their knees. They tried so hard to come back, but there was no way. And as hard as we tried to include them, they both seemed to be forgotten that year, the year we won the national championship. Maybe I've been outrageous ever since. I have a fear of being forgotten.

That's why I'll tell my kid to feel lucky for what he's got. I feel lucky that I had my parents to guide me. It's amazing, but a lot of people just assume I either (a) don't have parents and was sort of dropped here by an alien spacecraft or (b) don't talk to my parents because they must be ashamed of me. People look at me with their eyebrows all furrowed and say, "What must your mother and father think of you, son?" I always say, "I don't know, but I know if I was as ugly as you I wouldn't think much of *your* mother and father."

But my parents are proud as hell of me and that's the highlight of my life. My dad's a nut about me. He's got a scrapbook from every year that I've done anything. Do you know how many articles have been written about me? He's got them all. If somebody wrote it, he's got it.

He's not my coach anymore, but I still pull power from him when I'm on the field. I can be playing in Seattle and he can be in Irving and I can pull energy from him. My folks got me what I have today. They gave me the drive to win. There's no way I can pay them back, but I can try. I'm buying them a brand-new house in Plano, a ritzy section of Dallas. Not that they need much money. They're both professionals. They're going to keep their old one and let my sister move into it.

Right now, she's not so lucky. But I am. For every one time I've gotten my tit caught in the wringer, I've got ten thousand things go my way. Even though I have to spend half my time defending something nobody should have to defend—the right to be yourself—I've also gotten through to some people and had more fun than the law should allow. And best of all, I'm never, *ever* bored.

I remember one time Gary and I were coming out of court after having lost on the jersey thing. I was pissed and he was pissed. We were sort of just staring down at our shoes, grumbling. Then, all of a sudden, this old derelict we didn't even see hollers at us with the worst wino breath imaginable, "Hey, Boz! Get a *real* job!"

I just stopped and looked at him. I was about to say, "Oh, you got a *real* good job, don't you? Holding up that trash can. Nice. Have you taken a shower this month? Would you recognize a comb if you saw one? Do you know what the word 'deodorant' means?"

But then I started to laugh because I decided that old home boy was right. I *didn't* have a real job. What I do isn't a real job. What I'm planning on doing doesn't sound much like a real job either—reading scripts and walking to the mailbox for royalty checks. Who needs a real job anyway? Screw nine-to-five. Being a responsible cog in society is way overrated anyway, right, home boy?

So I'm carrying on with one of the world's great setups. And if I don't see you on the football field, I'll see you at the movies. I'll be the one in the Ferrari, laughing my ass off and riding into the sunset with the beautiful babe. And by the way, the license plate will read: 44.

Later!

CHAPTER 16

The World's Largest Book-Eating Party

OK, it's later. A year later. And a few small things have happened since I signed off. Like people waiting for me at the Oklahoma border with buckets of tar. Like Barry Switzer ripping me like I was Ted Bundy. Like me, Mr. Never-Miss-A-Game getting carved up by doctors twice in one season. Like Chuck Knox barring me from my own sideline.

Couldn't we just fax 1988 to hell or something?

The book—the one you have in your paws—came out in early August 1988, and was only mildly controversial, sort of the way Roseanne Barr is only mildly fat. You could have wallpapered your living room in the headlines alone:

BOZ ALLEGES COCAINE USE AT OU

BOZ SAYS OU PLAYERS WERE ARMED

BOZ SAYS ANARCHY RULES OU

Not that any of that wasn't true. In fact, all of it was true—the cocaine use, the weapons, the fat-cat lifestyle, the see-no-evil attitude—not to mention all the stuff we left out. I shudder to think what the state

279

of Oklahoma would've done if we'd have kept some of that stuff in.

THOUSANDS SEE FIRST LYNCHING IN YEARS

As it was, OU wasn't exactly setting up book-signing parties for me. Switzer went into the hall where all the pictures of OU All-Americans hang and took mine down. Does this mean I have to return my letter jacket?

Then Switzer denied everything: the money, the cocaine, the guns, the lawlessness, the if-you-can-play-you-can-do-anything-you-want mind-set, everything. And when the King had spoken, his subjects followed. The rest of Oklahoma started calling me a liar, a hypocrite, and a scumbag. They called me everything but a Texas fan.

But a funny thing happened to all those people who said I was full of it. They started picking up their morning newspapers and seeing it replayed again in black and white. A little ketchup goes nice with those hardcover-book pages, folks.

Remember the part about Buster Rhymes and his heavy artillery? Five months after the book came out, one of OU's starting cornerbacks, Jerry Parks, shot his teammate, Zarak Peters, with a gun in the football dorm. Now, where do you think those fun-lovin' young men happened upon firearms like that? If somebody had listened to me, maybe Zarak Peters wouldn't have a hole where no hole is supposed to be.

Remember the part about seeing some of my own teammates freebasing cocaine on the day of the game? Six months after the book came out, OU's starting quarterback, Charles Thompson, was busted by the FBI on charges that he sold 17 grams of cocaine to undercover cops. What do you know about that? Cocaine, right there among the athletes, just like it is right there among the rest of the students. Even Vinny Testaverde wouldn't admit to reporters what he'd told me, that there was a cocaine problem among the players at the University of Miami. Yet when Reggie Sutton, an ex-Miami player, ends up in cocaine rehabilitation with the New Orleans Saints, everybody's surprised.

Remember the part about alumni who give players money, fans who buy their tickets, restaurant owners who pick up their meals and store owners who give stuff away? Well, two months after the book came out, my teammate Keith Jackson admitted he received cash from alumni while at OU. Then the NCAA put OU on three years probation. The NCAA wrote that Switzer and the university had "failed to exercise supervisory control" over the football program. First time the NCAA had ever been right.

Remember how fond I was of His Dishonor, OU president Frank Horton? Well, just after the book came out, he left. Frankie says he left for a better job—Toledo. If Toledo is a better job, then North Dakota is a vacation paradise.

Remember how I said it was unfair for the goons at the NCAA to test for steroids when your body is totally dehydrated, like mine was? Well, even before the book came out, white-hat guys like Bobby Knight, John Thompson and Dean Smith were hollering about it, too. Seems the NCAA was testing players after games, when their bodies were dehydrated. The dial tones at the NCAA said, "Duh, yeah, maybe we should look into it.'' What do you have to do to get listened to in America, throw chairs across basketball courts?

And to think we took a lot of stuff out of the book because we thought it would be too outrageous for people to believe. After what's happened at OU lately, people are ready to hear everything.

A lot of it has to do with Hell Hall—the Bud Wilkinson athletic dorm. One thing that hasn't come out is how much gambling there was in the dorm. On most any night you could go downstairs and find guys playing pool for $20 a game—all night long— or go upstairs and find a good craps game or two going on. I never understood craps myself—some guy throwing dice, another guy picking it up before it stopped and everybody reaching for their money all at once. But a lot of guys seemed to like it— enough to put big money on the line. Put it this way, I never saw a $1 bill in any of those games. One time, one of my more thick-walleted buddies told me he'd lost $500 the night before playing craps. I'm glad I never learned that game.

Don't even ask why the crap games were never stopped. Why should they be? OU never stopped us from doing anything in that dorm. That's the whole reason schools keep athletic dorms, to keep everything in one place, under one roof. They know the players will recreate the last days of Saigon in there, yeah, but they know the coaches can keep it covered up there, too. ''Don't worry, Officer. Everything is under control. We've almost got the Ferrari out of the hall.''

Nobody ever came by that dorm to police us. The most abused rule in college history may be the midnight curfew they used to have for girls to be out of the rooms. Hell, lots of times, the girls didn't even start coming until after midnight.

But the three-on-one rape charges shocked me and I think it shocked the people of Oklahoma. So did the news about all the guns. It shouldn't have. I would say 50 to 60 percent of the dorm rooms had at least one weapon in them. Most of them were for hunting, but there were other uses, too. I knew guys who, just for kicks, would lean out their windows and pick off a pigeon or two. Used to scare hell out of the poor saps underneath trying to go to class. It's a little unnerving to have a dead pigeon land on your Biology 101 book. Some of my friends used to get a charge out of seeing if they could hit Dale Hall Tower, about a half a mile away, with a .22. They could.

The drugs got too serious sometimes. I don't know how many guys dealt, but let's just say there were rooms you knew to stay the hell out of—and guys to stay away from. One time during my sophomore year, I was pulling my car out of the fieldhouse parking lot, when a certain teammate comes running full-speed right at me. I roll down my window to see what was up and he says, "Boz, I need a ride! These guys are chasing me!" I look behind me and I see three derelicts coming at my car, holding guns.

"Sorry, Dude," I said, "you're on your own." I put it in "D" and I was history. Next thing I know, he's outrunning my car and derelicts are climbing out of pine trees and digging out of trash cans, all armed. They were FBI narcs and they busted him right in the middle of the street, facedown.

And you know what? That story never made the

papers. I never did hear anything about it again, except the kid was gone.

Hearing about Thompson was a sad thing. When he was a freshman, he was as nice a kid as you'd want to meet. Here was this quiet, shy kid from Lawton, Oklahoma, who just wanted to play football. And now look at him. You can't tell me it's only the kids Switzer recruits. Sometimes it's what happens to good kids once they get there. You throw a good kid in with bad kids and you can see what happens. They're gods. They can do anything they want. Forget laws, morals, what's right and wrong.

They were treated like gods, too. Sometimes the trips were set up for guys to fly down to Amarillo, Texas, or some little town and just sign autographs and get up at some coaching seminar and answer questions. That paid $1500 to $2500, probably donated by some alumni, and all of it considered very illegal by the NCAA. But the point is, if no one else cared about laws, why should the players?

That's how it was with drug testing, too. Guys would piss in the bottle, then throw sugar in there to screw up the test. And even when guys would test positive, plenty of times nothing would happen.

I guess people will get all tight in the underwear when they read that, but all of it's true, just like last time. So many things were reproven true in the book they should just make it the OU manual: prerequisite reading for all freshmen. Now, when I tell you that your ass is about to be flatter than a fifty-cent piece, you'll start looking out for 18-wheelers.

Still, even though I've been vindicated, it pisses me off how people reacted to the book in the first place: with minds closed and mouths wide open.

People would come up to me and say, "You hypocrite. First you take all that free stuff and then you go and blab about it in your book. You sicked the NCAA on us."

That's all bull and everybody with the IQ of a lugnut knows it. First of all, the NCAA was investigating OU three months before the book came out. Second of all, I wasn't blabbing anything. Nothing I wrote could be traced to anybody. Nothing I wrote *has* ever been traced to anybody, and I did it that way on purpose. In fact, the NCAA asked both my father and I to testify against OU and we told them to shove it up their briefcases. I still love OU and I still love the state of Oklahoma.

Seriously, even after what Switzer said about me— "Brian Bosworth is no longer welcome here," and "I feel like he just stuck a knife in my back,"—I still don't hate him. Even though it was Switzer's fingerprints on the knife in the first place. He was the one who stuck it up to the handle in my back when he kicked me off the team for a 10-second T-shirt mistake.

The book wasn't meant to be a *60 Minutes* rip job on OU. It wasn't some white paper on OU. It was a white paper on how screwed up the NCAA is, and how screwed up the rules are that force players to accept free stuff in order to live like every other English major and sociology nerd on campus, to be able to buy a pizza once in a while or take their girlfriends to a movie.

The solution to all this is so simple if the NCAA would just read my lips. Just take money from the TV packages and give it to the players this way: freshmen get $100 a month, sophomores $200, juniors $300, seniors $400, redshirt seniors $500. The system is constant all over the country for Division I schools. A Missouri junior gets the same as a Miami junior. This not only takes away the advantage the cheaters have—no recruit would risk becoming ineligible if he knows he's going to get a little spending money—but it might keep some kids out of trouble. Maybe if Charles Thompson had $100 bucks a month spending money, he wouldn't have been allegedly jacking around with cocaine in the first place.

Oklahoma needs to do one more thing to clean things up: Hire John Blake.*

When I was at OU, John was the buffer between Switzer and the players. John was the guy players could trust, the one they could go to with their problems without worrying that John was going to go straight to Switzer, the one who could sniff out trouble and put a stop to it before it got too big. When he left after my junior season to take a better job at Tulsa, the players went wild. When John left, there was only one black assistant coach left, and none that the players could really go to. John kept me out of trouble and he kept a lot of players out of trouble.

I still talk to John a lot, and I think if Switzer offered him the right job, he'd be back in a minute. Switzer should think hard about it. John might keep him from getting fired.

Maybe this time people will want to hear the message instead of trying to kill the messenger, especially when the messenger is me.

Nobody much wanted to hear about the book in

---

*At the time this chapter went to press, John Blake was still employed by the University of Tulsa. —Editor

Seattle, either, especially my wonderful teammate, Bryan Millard, the offensive lineman who is making terrific progress lately. He's learning to walk erect. I guess Bry didn't like some of the things I said about him in the book, especially the fact that he dresses the way Spam looks. One day, Sam Merriman and Dave Wyman and I are sitting around the training table laughing at the shirt Millard was wearing. Swear to God, Millard's shirt was exactly the same as our tablecloth.

So Wyman says, "Where'd you get that shirt, Millard? Picnics R Us?"

I almost choked on my mashed potatoes. Unfortunately, Millard thought I said it.

He came over looking to fight. "Just because I wear zipper jeans doesn't make me a geek," he said.

"No," I said, "but the fact that you shop at the Big and Dork shop does."

He started pushing chairs around and yelling unmentionables, telling me to step outside, but Merriman got him to chill out before anything happened.

Most of the guys took the book pretty well. No, my problem in Seattle during the '88 season wasn't the book, it was my body. It came apart. The warranty expired. I unraveled like a K-Mart sweater.

All through the off-season, my shoulder felt like somebody was using a Skill saw on it. It had always hurt before, but now it was getting ridiculous. I couldn't comb my hair (and you *know* that's serious), couldn't put a coat on without help, couldn't lift weights, couldn't get a half gallon of milk off the top shelf of the refrigerator. If I'd have lived on the 40th floor of an apartment building, I'd have had to push the button for 20 and walk the rest of the way up. They should've let me park in the handicapped spots.

So the doctors started giving me those big, hairy anti-inflammatory cortisone shots again, the ones where they stick it in your shoulder and you feel it in your finger. Unfortunately, you can only get three in a year or you turn into The Elephant Man or John Elway or something. I got one before camp, then halfway through camp, then another just before the opening game in Denver against the Elways, in which we stuck it to my favorite NFL star, Mr. Ed.

But that was my last shot and, therefore, my last decent game. Even halfway through it, my shoulder was barking. If it hadn't been for Denver's munchkin offensive line, I might not have made a tackle that second half. By the next week, in Kansas City, my arm was just a limp rag hanging there. I looked like The Fugitive. I couldn't wrap up anybody. I made a lot of tackles just throwing my head and one arm in there. But if they went to the other side, I was beaten like an egg yolk.

I tried to keep on playing but it was useless. You could've put a "yield" sign up instead of me and it would've done more good. So, I had our team surgeon, Dr. Pierce Scranton, cut it up. Afterwards, Scranton said to me, "You take a couple weeks rest and you'll be good as new." Maybe he really believed that, but I believe that most NFL doctors tell you what the coach wants you to hear.

And so, like a fool, I played on it again right away. I probably played two games on it I shouldn't have and finally, the pain was so ridiculous and the arm so useless, I went and saw a shoulder expert, Dr. Frank Jobe, in Los Angeles. He said, "Look, that's a career-threatening injury. You need to rest it for the rest of the season.'' So I went back and told Chuck, ''Look, I'm sitting out until I get this thing 100 percent better. I'm not going to jeopardize my future.''

Meanwhile, I was going insane. Everybody on the team up to and including the janitor wanted to know when I was coming back. And people in doctors' offices, too. If I heard it once, I heard it a thousand times: ''How's the shoulder coming, Boz?'' I wonder how people would like it if I bothered them in doctors' waiting rooms? ''So, how's the impotency coming, Morty?''

Most of the players resented my taking myself out, as if they knew what was wrong. Most players are a lot like coaches: they only care about one thing, you getting your ass on the field *today*, so they can make a bigger check at the end of the season. So what if you won't be around for the eight seasons after that?

Actually, Chuck was pretty good about my injury. He seemed to care about what happened to me over the long haul. But what he did to me while I was injured I thought was horseshit. All of a sudden, he decided the injured players couldn't stand on the sideline. He said it was some league rule: no injured players on the sideline. But I knew it was total bullshit. The first game he wouldn't let me come to was against the Raiders on *Monday Night Football*. The nation sees two Raiders, Todd Christiansen and Howie Long, both injured, standing on the Raiders sideline. And it was a *road* game for them. And it was the same for every other team. What is Joe Six-pack sitting in Boise supposed to think about me? That I don't give a damn, that's what.

Then, to make matters even worse, somebody started this brilliant rumor that I was addicted to pain pills and going to a drug rehab center every day. The center they were talking about was almost a three-hour drive from Seattle, which meant that I was driving six hours a day, since I was at practice every day. Maybe I was addicted to driving. I guess somebody had seen a white Corvette there and assumed it was mine. Right. There's only one in the state. Besides, by then I was driving a black Corvette.

Anyway, we barely made the playoffs at 9–7 and mostly because the Elways and the Raiders were gagging left and right. Then we play our asses off but lose to the eventual Super Bowl entrants, Cincinnati. By the way, the guy who came in for me, Darren Commeaux, played great.

Then, just for added excitement, I found out my knee needed surgery in January. So I went to Scranton. He took out a cyst and a bone spur that was sticking out about an inch and a half. I guess he did a fine job. But I know one thing, if it had been during the season, most team doctors would have said, "Ahh, it's just a nick. Get some Bactein on it and get back in there." All of which added up to a season worth forgetting.

Listen, I still get jacked up playing football, but I'll admit, all the hypocrisy of it, all the big-business of it, all the pettiness of it has taken away some of my love for it. I liked football better when it was still a game, not a W-2 form.

I know one thing. I want to leave the game before it leaves me. I don't want to be some guy walking out with his pink slip and half a knee. I don't want to limp away. I think Steve Largent, who has proven to be the greatest receiver of all time, should have retired last year with all his injuries. I'm afraid the only reason Steve is playing is because the fans want to see him pass Don Maynard in touchdowns. Maybe he thinks the fans deserve to see him do it. Me, I'm more concerned about Steve Largent's health than about some number somebody prints in *The Sporting News*. I want to live to be an old, healthy man, not an unhealthy half a man.

Then again, no matter how old I live to be, even if I live to be so old that Willard Scott starts mentioning me during the weather, I can always take satisfaction in knowing one thing.

I'll never look as bad as Rozelle.

HIGH-TECH ADVENTURES BY
BESTSELLING AUTHORS

__**TEAM YANKEE** by Harold Coyle
  0-425-11042-7/$4.95
Live the first two weeks of World War III through the eyes of tank team commander Captain Sean Bannon, as he and his soldiers blast their way across the war-torn plains of Europe.

__**AMBUSH AT OSIRAK** by Herbert Crowder
  0-515-09932-5/$4.50
Israel is poised to attack the Iraqi nuclear production plant at Osirak. But the Soviets have supplied Iraq with the ultimate super-weapon . . . and the means to wage nuclear war.

__**SWEETWATER GUNSLINGER 201** by Lt.
  Commander William H. LaBarge and Robert
  Lawrence Holt 1-55773-191-8/$4.50
Jet jockeys Sweetwater and Sundance are the most outrageous pilots in the skies. Testing the limits of their F-14s and their commanding officers, these boys won't let anything get in the way of their fun!

__**WILDCAT** by Craig Thomas 0-515-10186-9/$4.95
Crossing the globe from Moscow to London to East Berlin to Katmandu, the bestselling author of *Winter Hawk* delivers edge-of-the-seat suspense spiked with state-of-the-art espionage gadgetry. (On sale in November '89)

231